OHCHR

D1520882

Teaching
Human Rights

Practical activities for primary and secondary schools

United Nations
New York and
Geneva, 2004

HR/PUB/2004/2

UNITED NATIONS PUBLICATION
Sales No. E.03.XIV.3
ISBN 92-1-154149-2

CREDIT

Photos
Cover and first page: UN/DPI, UN/DPI, UNESCO/A. Abbé, UN/DPI – p. 8-9: UNESCO/A. Abbé – p. 11: UNICEF/HQ93-1919/G. Pirozzi – p. 14: UNICEF/HQ97-0448/J. Horner – p. 19: UN/DPI – p. 20: UN/DPI – p. 23: UNESCO/O. Pasquiers – p. 24: UNESCO/O. Pasquiers – p. 30-31: UNESCO/P. Waeles – p. 48-49: UN/DPI – p. 102-103: UNICEF/HQ97-0448/J. Horner – p. 110-111: UNESCO/O. Pasquiers – p. 140-141: UNESCO/D. Roger – p. 146-147: UNESCO/O. Pasquiers – p. 156-157: UNESCO/D. Roger – Back cover: UNESCO/D. Roger, UNESCO/D. Roger, UNICEF/HQ93-1919/G. Pirozzi, UNESCO/O. Pasquiers, UN/DPI, UNESCO/A. Abbé

Illustrations
F. Sterpin

Graphic design
Louma productions

Foreword

ABC: Teaching Human Rights - Practical activities for primary and secondary schools talks about us as human beings. It talks about the process of teaching and learning the significance of the inherent "dignity and worth of the human person" which is the "foundation of freedom, justice and peace in the world" (Universal Declaration of Human Rights, preamble). And it talks about the rights that belong to us all.

These are not just lessons for the classroom but lessons for life – of immediate relevance to our daily life and experience. In this sense, human rights education means not only teaching and learning *about* human rights, but also *for* human rights: its fundamental role is to empower individuals to defend their own rights and those of others. This empowerment constitutes an important investment for the future, aimed at achieving a just society in which all human rights of all persons are valued and respected.

This booklet is a practical contribution by my Office to the United Nations Decade for Human Rights Education (1995-2004), during which Governments, international organizations, non-governmental organizations, professional associations, all sectors of civil society and individuals have been especially encouraged to establish partnerships and to concentrate efforts for human rights education. The Decade provides us with a global common framework in which we can work together; indeed, the realization of human rights is our common responsibility, and its achievement is entirely dependent on the contribution that each and everyone will be willing to make. I hope that this booklet and other initiatives based on it will lead many individuals who work as teachers and educators around the world to be positive agents of change.

I wish to extend thanks to the individuals and organizations who supported my Office in the preparation of this booklet, in particular Ralph Pettman, who developed the first 1989 edition; Nancy Flowers, who worked on the revision and updating of that edition; and Margot Brown, Felisa Tibbitts and the UNESCO Division for the Promotion of Quality Education, who provided useful comments and suggestions for improvement.

Sergio Vieira de Mello
United Nations High Commissioner for Human Rights
March 2003

Contents

Abbreviations

CEDAW	Convention on the Elimination of All Forms of Discrimination against Women
CRC	Convention on the Rights of the Child
FAO	Food and Agriculture Organization of the United Nations
ICERD	International Convention on the Elimination of All Forms of Racial Discrimination
ICRC	International Committee of the Red Cross
ILO	International Labour Organization
OHCHR	Office of the United Nations High Commissioner for Human Rights
UDHR	Universal Declaration of Human Rights
UNDP	United Nations Development Programme
UNEP	United Nations Environment Programme
UNESCO	United Nations Educational, Scientific and Cultural Organization
UNHCR	Office of the United Nations High Commissioner for Refugees
UNICEF	United Nations Children's Fund
WHO	World Health Organization

Introduction

Using *ABC: Teaching Human Rights*

ABC: Teaching Human Rights aims to serve as a user-friendly tool for human rights education and a multi-coloured umbrella covering a number of basic human rights areas. It offers practical advice to teachers and other educators who want to foster human rights awareness and action among primary and secondary school children, including suggestions for developing learning activities. It is not meant to place an extra burden on an already overloaded curriculum but to assist in infusing human rights issues into subjects already taught in schools.

There has been much research into how children and young people develop judgements as they grow. Not every class member may be able to grasp fully every human rights principle: pressing students to understand right from the beginning may pre-empt the honest expression of what they think or feel and may even halt further progress. This booklet assumes that all human beings benefit from the chance to explore rights issues, and that by the age of ten years or so, students given such a chance have a capacity for lively and profound reflection far beyond that usually expected. The suggested activities require few extra materials. Instead they call on the richest resource all teachers have to work with – their students and their experiences in everyday life.

Chapter One lays out principal human rights concepts and the fundamentals of human rights education. It reviews basic content and methodologies and elaborates on participatory techniques.

Chapter Two is intended for primary school teachers, offering suggestions for nurturing younger children's sense of their own worth and that of others through materials that evoke the human rights principles of human dignity and equality.

Chapter Three contains activities for upper primary and secondary school students that are of a more sophisticated nature and deal with current issues.

The activities in **Chapter Two** and **Chapter Three** are intended to give students a more profound awareness and understanding of human rights issues around the world and in their own classroom and community. They aim at stimulating independent thinking and research and building skills for active citizenship in a democracy. It is also important for students to enjoy the activities. It can be better to abandon or interrupt an activity if students put up too much resistance.

Each activity is followed by a reference to articles of the *Universal Declaration of Human Rights* and the *Convention on the Rights of the Child*, two United Nations instruments that are introduced in **Chapter One** and reproduced respectively in **Annex 1** and **Annex 2**. The references aim at highlighting the provisions that served as a source of inspiration for each activity; however, the activities may not necessarily reflect the full scope and extent of the rights contained in the above-mentioned instruments, as recognized by international law. **Annex 3** contains a brief introduction to the terminology used in this body of law.

ABC: Teaching Human Rights is one of the many resources available worldwide for furthering human rights education with schoolchildren. It can be a starting point for further research and study on the subject with a view to developing culturally appropriate materials at all teaching levels, and can be used in conjunction with or supplemented by other materials developed by local actors (governmental agencies, national human rights institutions, non-governmental organizations and other civil society entities), to which teachers and users in general may also turn for assistance and support.

A selection of other classroom resources produced at the international and regional levels is included in **Annex 5**; other materials, including various documents mentioned in the text, can also be obtained from, inter alia, the organizations mentioned in **Annex 4** and their local offices.

Chapter One

Fundamentals of Human Rights Education

Human rights may be generally defined as those rights which are inherent in our nature and without which we cannot live as human beings. Human rights and fundamental freedoms allow us to develop fully and use our human qualities, our intelligence, our talents and our conscience and to satisfy our spiritual and other needs. They are based on humankind's increasing demand for a life in which the inherent dignity and worth of each human being are accorded respect and protection. Their denial is not only an individual and personal tragedy but also creates conditions of social and political unrest, sowing the seeds of violence and conflict within and between societies and nations.

The development of the human rights framework

The history of human rights has been shaped by all major world events and by the struggle for dignity, freedom and equality everywhere. Yet it was only with the establishment of the United Nations that human rights finally achieved formal, universal recognition.

The turmoil and atrocities of the Second World War and the growing struggle of colonial nations for independence prompted the countries of the world to create a forum to deal with some of the war's consequences and, in particular, to prevent the recurrence of such appalling events. This forum was the United Nations.

When the United Nations was founded in 1945, it reaffirmed the faith in human rights of all the peoples taking part. Human rights were cited in the founding Charter as central to their concerns and have remained so ever since.

One of the first major achievements of the newly formed United Nations was the Universal Declaration of Human Rights (UDHR),[1] adopted by the United Nations General Assembly on 10 December 1948. This powerful instrument continues to exert an enormous impact on people's lives all over the world. It was the first time in history that a document considered to have universal value was adopted by an international organization. It was also the first time that human rights and fundamental freedoms were set forth in such detail.

There was broad-based international support for the Declaration when it was adopted. Although the fifty-eight Member States that constituted the United Nations at that time varied in terms of their ideology, political system, religious and cultural background, and patterns of socio-economic development, the Universal Declaration of Human Rights represented a common statement of shared goals and aspirations – a vision of the world as the international community would like it to be.

The Declaration recognizes that the "inherent dignity ... of all members of the human family is the foundation of freedom, justice and peace in the world" and is linked to the recogni-

---

[1] For the full text and simplified version of the *Universal Declaration of Human Rights*, see annex 1.

tion of the fundamental rights to which every human being aspires, namely the right to life, liberty and security of person; the right to an adequate standard of living; the right to seek and to enjoy in other countries asylum from persecution; the right to own property; the right to freedom of opinion and expression; the right to education; the right to freedom of thought, conscience and religion; and the right to freedom from torture and degrading treatment, among others. These are inherent rights to be enjoyed by all inhabitants of the global village (women, men, children and all groups in society, whether disadvantaged or not) and not "gifts" to be withdrawn, withheld or granted at someone's whim or will.

Eleanor Roosevelt, who chaired the United Nations Commission on Human Rights in its early years, emphasized both the universality of these rights and the responsibility they entail when she asked:

Where, after all, do universal human rights begin? In small places, close to home – so close and so small that they cannot be seen on any maps of the world. Yet they are the world of the individual person; the neighbourhood he lives in; the school or college he attends; the factory, farm or office where he works. Such are the places where every man, woman and child seeks equal justice, equal opportunity, equal dignity without discrimination. Unless these rights have meaning there, they have little meaning anywhere. Without concerned citizen action to uphold them close to home, we shall look in vain for progress in the larger world.[2]

[2] Eleanor Roosevelt, "In Our Hands" (1958 speech delivered on the tenth anniversary of the Universal Declaration of Human Rights).

On the occasion of the fiftieth anniversary of the Universal Declaration of Human Rights in 1998, Mary Robinson, United Nations High Commissioner for Human Rights, called it "one of the great aspirational documents of our human history". It has served as the model for many national constitutions and has truly become the most universal of all instruments, having been translated into more languages than any other.[3]

The Declaration has inspired a large number of subsequent human rights instruments, which together constitute the international law of human rights.[4] These instruments include the International Covenant on Economic, Social and Cultural Rights (1966) and the International Covenant on Civil and Political Rights (1966), treaties that are legally binding on the States that are parties to them. The Universal Declaration and the two Covenants constitute the International Bill of Human Rights.

The rights contained in the Declaration and the two Covenants have been further elaborated in other treaties such as the International Convention on the Elimination of All Forms of Racial Discrimination (1965), which declares dissemination of ideas based on racial superiority or hatred as being punishable by law, and the Convention on the Elimination of All Forms of Discrimination against Women (1979), prescribing measures to be taken to eliminate discrimination against women in political and public life, education, employment, health, marriage and the family.

Of particular importance to anyone involved with schools is the Convention on the Rights of the Child,[5] which lays down guarantees of the child's human rights. Adopted by the General Assembly in 1989, the Convention has been ratified by more countries than any other human rights treaty. In addition to guaranteeing children protection from harm and abuse and making special provision for their survival and welfare through, for example, health care, education and family life, it

[3] For more information on the Universal Declaration, including the text of the UDHR in more than 330 languages and dialects, see http://www.ohchr.org or contact the Office of the United Nations High Commissioner for Human Rights.

[4] For a brief introduction to international human rights law terminology, including some words used in this chapter such as "treaty", "convention", "protocol" and "ratification", see annex 3. For a full overview of international human rights instruments, see http://www.ohchr.org or contact the Office of the United Nations High Commissioner for Human Rights.

[5] For the full text and summarized version of the Convention on the Rights of the Child, see annex 2.

Chart of the Principal United Nations Human Rights Instruments

INTERNATIONAL BILL OF HUMAN RIGHTS Universal Declaration of Human Rights (UDHR), 1948				
International Covenant on Civil and Political Rights (ICCPR), 1966			International Covenant on Economic, Social and Cultural Rights (ICESCR), 1966	
Convention relating to the Status of Refugees, 1951	International Convention on the Elimination of All Forms of Racial Discrimination, 1965	Convention on the Elimination of All Forms of Discrimination against Women, 1979	Convention against Torture and Other Cruel, Inhuman or Degrading Treatment or Punishment, 1984	Convention on the Rights of the Child, 1989

accords them the right to participate in society and in decision-making that concerns them. Two Protocols to the Convention have recently been adopted, the Optional Protocol on the sale of children, child prostitution and child pornography and the Optional Protocol on the involvement of children in armed conflict (2000).

Promoting human rights

Since the adoption of the Universal Declaration of Human Rights, human rights have become central to the work of the United Nations. Emphasizing the universality of human rights, Secretary-General Kofi Annan stated on the fiftieth anniversary of the Declaration that "Human rights is foreign to no country and native to all nations" and that "without human rights no peace or prosperity will ever last".

Within the United Nations system, human rights are furthered by a myriad of different mechanisms and procedures: by working groups and committees; by reports, studies and statements; by conferences, plans and programmes; by decades for action; by research and training; by voluntary and trust funds; by assistance of many kinds at the global, regional and local levels; by specific measures taken; by

investigations conducted; and by the many procedures devised to promote and protect human rights.

Action to build a culture of human rights is also supported by United Nations specialized agencies, programmes and funds such as the United Nations Educational, Scientific and Cultural Organization (UNESCO), the United Nations Children's Fund (UNICEF), the Office of the United Nations High Commissioner for Refugees (UNHCR), the United Nations Development Programme (UNDP), the International Labour Organization (ILO) and the World Health Organization (WHO) and by relevant departments of the United Nations Secretariat such as the Office of the United Nations High Commissioner for Human Rights (OHCHR). Other international, regional and national bodies, both governmental and non-governmental, are also working to promote human rights.

At the World Conference on Human Rights held in Vienna, Austria, in 1993, 171 countries reiterated the universality, indivisibility and interdependence of human rights, and reaffirmed their commitment to the Universal Declaration of Human Rights. They adopted the Vienna Declaration and Programme of Action, which provides the new "framework of planning, dialogue and cooperation" to facilitate the adoption of a holistic approach to promoting human rights and to involve actors at the local, national and international levels.

The United Nations Decade for Human Rights Education (1995-2004)

Not least of these activities to promote human rights is human rights education. Since the adoption of the Universal Declaration, the General Assembly has called on Member States and all segments of society to disseminate this fundamental document and educate people about its content. The 1993 World Conference on Human Rights also reaffirmed the importance of education, training and public information.

In response to the appeal by the World Conference, the General Assembly, in 1994, proclaimed the period 1995 to 2004 the United Nations Decade for Human Rights Education. The Assembly affirmed that "human rights education should involve more than the provision of information and should constitute a comprehensive life-long process by which people at all levels in development and in all strata of society learn respect for the dignity of others and the means and methods of ensuring that respect in all societies".

The Plan of Action for the Decade provides a definition of the concept of human rights education as agreed by the international community, i.e. based on the provisions of international human rights instruments.[6] In accordance with those provisions, human rights education may be defined as "training, dissemination and information efforts aimed at the building of a universal culture of human rights through the imparting of knowledge and skills and the moulding of attitudes and directed to:

(a) The strengthening of respect for human rights and fundamental freedoms;

(b) The full development of the human personality and the sense of its dignity;

(c) The promotion of understanding, tolerance, gender equality and friendship among all nations, indigenous peoples and racial, national, ethnic, religious and linguistic groups;

---

[6] Including the Universal Declaration of Human Rights (art. 26.2), the International Covenant on Economic, Social and Cultural Rights (art. 13.1), the Convention on the Rights of the Child (art. 29.1) and the Vienna Declaration and Programme of Action (sect. D, paras. 78 82).

(d) The enabling of all persons to participate effectively in a free society;

(e) The furtherance of the activities of the United Nations for the maintenance of peace."[7]

The Decade's Plan of Action provides a strategy for furthering human rights education through the assessment of needs and the formulation of effective strategies; the building and strengthening of programmes and capacities at the international, regional, national and local levels; the coordinated development of materials; the strengthening of the role of the mass media; and the global dissemination of the Universal Declaration of Human Rights.

The process of human rights education in schools

A sustainable (in the long term), comprehensive and effective national strategy for infusing human rights education into educational systems may include various courses of action, such as:

• The incorporation of human rights education in national legislation regulating education in schools;

• The revision of curricula and textbooks;

• Preservice and inservice training for teachers to include training on human rights and human rights education methodologies;

• The organization of extracurricular activities, both based on schools and reaching out to the family and the community;

• The development of educational materials;

• The establishment of support networks of teachers and other professionals (from human rights groups, teachers' unions, non-governmental organizations or professional associations) and so on.

The concrete way in which this process takes place in each country depends on local educational systems which differ widely, not least in the degree of discretion teachers may exercise in setting their own teaching goals and meeting

---

[7] See United Nations document A/51/506/Add.1, appendix, para. 2 – available at http://www.ohchr.org or by contacting the Office of the United Nations High Commissioner for Human Rights.

Familiarization of children with human rights concepts - A step-by-step approach

Levels	Goals	Key concepts	Practices	Specific human rights problems	Human rights standards, systems and instruments
Early childhood					
Pre-school and lower primary school Ages 3-7	• Respect for self • Respect for parents and teachers • Respect for others	• Self • Community • Personal responsibility	• Duty • Fairness • Self-expression/listening • Cooperation/sharing • Small group work • Individual work • Understanding cause/effect • Empathy • Democracy • Conflict resolution	• Racism • Sexism • Unfairness • Hurting people (feelings, physically)	• Classroom rules • Family life • Community standards • Universal Declaration of Human Rights • Convention on the Rights of the Child
Later Childhood					
Upper primary school Ages 8-11	All the above plus: • Social responsibility • Citizenship • Distinguishing wants from needs, from rights	• Individual rights • Group rights • Freedom • Equality • Justice • Rule of law • Government • Security	• Valuing diversity • Fairness • Distinguishing between fact and opinion • Performing school or community service • Civic participation	• Discrimination/ prejudice • Poverty/hunger • Injustice • Ethnocentrism • Egocentrism • Passivity	• History of human rights • Local, national legal systems • Local and national history in human rights terms • UNESCO, UNICEF • Non-governmental organizations (NGOs)
Adolescence					
Lower secondary school Ages 12-14	All the above plus: • Knowledge of specific human rights	• International law • World peace • World development • World political economy • World ecology	• Understanding other points of view • Citing evidence in support of ideas • Doing research / gathering information • Sharing information	• Ignorance • Apathy • Cynicism • Political repression • Colonialism/imperialism • Economic globalization • Environmental degradation	• United Nations Covenants • Elimination of racism • Elimination of sexism • United Nations High Commissioner for Refugees • Regional human rights conventions
Youth					
Upper secondary school Ages 15-17	All the above plus: • Knowledge of human rights as universal standards • Integration of human rights into personal awareness and behaviour	• Moral inclusion/exclusion • Moral responsibility/ literacy	• Participation in civic organizations • Fulfilling civic responsibilities • Civic disobedience	• Genocide • Torture • War crimes etc.	• Geneva Conventions • Specialized conventions • Evolving human rights standards

them. The teacher will always be the key person, however, in getting new initiatives to work. The teacher therefore carries a great responsibility for communication of the human rights message. Opportunities to do this may vary: human rights themes may be infused into existing school subjects, such as history, civics, literature, art, geography, languages and scientific subjects, or may have a specific course allocated to them; human rights education may also be pursued through less formal education arenas within and outside schools such as after-school activities, clubs and youth forums.

Ideally, a human rights culture should be built into the whole curriculum (yet in practice, particularly at secondary level, it is usually treated piecemeal, as part of the established curriculum in the social and economic sciences and the humanities).

In the classroom, human rights education should be developed with due attention to the developmental stage of children and their social and cultural contexts in order to make human rights principles meaningful to them. For example, human rights education for younger children could emphasize the development of self-esteem and empathy and a classroom culture supportive of human rights principles. Although young children are able to grasp the underlying principles of basic human rights instruments, the more complex content of human rights documents may be more appropriate to older learners with better developed capacities for concept development and analytical reasoning. The table on p. 17 reflects a matrix proposing the progressive introduction of children to human rights concepts depending on their age. The proposal is not meant to be prescriptive but only to provide an example, which was developed and discussed by human rights education practitioners gathered in Geneva in 1997.

Content for human rights education

The history of human rights tells a detailed story of efforts made to define the basic dignity and worth of the human being and his or her most fundamental entitlements. These efforts continue to this day. The teacher will want to include

an account of this history as an essential part of human rights teaching, and it can be made progressively more sophisticated as students mature. The fight for civil and political rights, the campaign to abolish slavery, the struggle for economic and social justice, the achievement of the Universal Declaration of Human Rights and the two subsequent Covenants, and all the conventions and declarations that followed, especially the Convention on the Rights of the Child – all these topics provide a basic legal and normative framework.

The core content of human rights education in schools is the Universal Declaration of Human Rights and the Convention on the Rights of the Child. These documents – which have received universal recognition, as explained above – provide principles and ideas with which to assess experience and build a school culture that values human rights. The rights they embody are universal, meaning that all human beings are entitled to them, on an equal basis; they are indivisible, meaning there is no hierarchy of rights, i.e. no right can be ranked as "non-essential" or "less important" than another. Instead human rights are interdependent, part of a complementary framework. For example, your right to participate in government is directly affected by your right to express yourself, to form associations, to get an education and even to obtain the necessities of life. Each human right is necessary and each is interrelated to all others.

However, even taught with the greatest skill and care, documents and history alone cannot bring human rights to life in the classroom. Nor does working through the Universal Declaration or the Convention on the Rights of the Child, pointing out the rationale for each article, teach the meaning of these articles in people's lives. "Facts" and "fundamentals", even the best-selected ones, are not enough to build a culture of human rights. For these documents to have more than intellectual significance, students need to approach them from the perspective of their real-life experience and grapple with them in terms of their own understanding of justice, freedom and equity.

Teaching *about* and *for* human rights

Research has shown that some upper primary and secondary school students sometimes suffer from a lack of confidence that limits their ability to socialize with others. It is difficult to care about someone else's rights when you do not expect to have any yourself. Where this is the case, teaching for

human rights could require going back to the beginning and teaching confidence and tolerance first, as proposed in Chapter Two of this booklet. The trust exercises, in the same chapter, can be used with any group and help to establish a good classroom climate, which is crucial for human rights education. These activities can be repeated (with suitable variations) to settle students into activities that require group cooperation. They can also foster the human capacity for sympathy, which is fragile and contingent but nonetheless real, and confirm the fact that no person is more of a human being than another and no person is less.

Already implicit above is the idea – central to this booklet – that teaching *about* human rights is not enough. The teacher will want to begin, and never to finish, teaching *for* human rights. For this reason the largest part of this text consists of activities. These create opportunities for students and teachers first to examine the basic elements that make up human rights – life, justice, freedom, equality and the destructive character of deprivation, suffering and pain – and then to use them to work out what they truly think and feel about a wide range of real-world issues.

The focus of human rights education is not just outward on external issues and events but also inward on personal values, attitudes and behaviour. To affect behaviour and inspire a sense of responsibility for human rights, human rights education uses participatory methodologies that emphasize independent research, analysis and critical thinking.

Rights and responsibilities

For the basic principles of a human rights culture to survive, people must continue to see a point in defending them: "I have a right to this. It is not just what I want, or need. It is my right. There is a responsibility to be met." But rights stand only by the reasons given for them and the reasons must be good ones. Unless people have the chance to work out such reasons for themselves – and where better than at school? – they will not claim their rights when they are withheld or taken away, or feel responsibility to defend the rights of others. We have to see for ourselves why rights are so important, for this in turn fosters responsibility.

It is, of course, possible to proceed the other way around: to teach for human rights in terms of responsibilities and obligations first. But again, teachers will want to do more than tell students what they ought to be doing. To bring these ideas alive, they will create opportunities for students to truly understand and accept such social responsibilities. Teachers and students will then have the principles and skills required to resolve the inevitable conflicts of responsibilities, obligations or rights when they arise.

Because these points of conflict can also provide useful insights, they should be welcomed. They make the teaching of human rights dynamic and relevant. Conflict offers the sort of learning opportunities that encourage students to face contrasts creatively, without fear, and to seek their own ways of resolving them.

Teaching and preaching: action speaks louder than words

The fact that the Universal Declaration of Human Rights and the Convention on the Rights of the Child have virtual global validity and applicability is very important for teachers. By promoting universal human rights standards, the teacher can honestly say that he or she is not preaching. Teachers have a second challenge, however: to teach in such a way as to respect human rights in the classroom and the school environment itself. For learning to have practical benefit, students need not only to learn about human rights but to learn in an environment that models them.

This means avoiding any hypocrisy. At its simplest, hypocrisy refers to situations where what a teacher is teaching is clearly at odds with how he or she is teaching it. For example: "Today we are going to talk about freedom of expression – shut up in the back row!" In such circumstances, students will learn mostly about power, and considerably less about human rights. As students spend a good deal of time studying teachers and can develop a good understanding of teachers' beliefs, a teacher who behaves unjustly or abusively will have little positive effect. Often, because of a desire to please, students may try to mirror a teacher's personal views without thinking for themselves. This may be a reason, at the beginning at least, for teachers not to express their own ideas. At its most complex, hypocrisy raises profound questions about how to protect and promote the human dignity of both teachers and students in a classroom, in a school and within society at large.

The "human rights climate" within schools and classrooms should rest on reciprocal respect between all the actors involved. Accordingly, the way in which decision-making processes take place, methods for resolving conflicts and administering discipline, and the relationship within and among all actors constitute key contributing factors.

Ultimately teachers need to explore ways to involve not only students, school administrators, education authorities and parents in human rights education but also the whole community. In this way teaching for human rights can reach from the classroom into the community to the benefit of both. All concerned will be able to discuss universal values and their relation to reality and to recognize that schools can be part of the solution to basic human rights problems.

As far as the students are concerned, negotiating a set of classroom rules and responsibilities is a long-tested and most effective way to begin (see the activity *Creating classroom rules* in Chapter Two). Teaching practices that are compatible

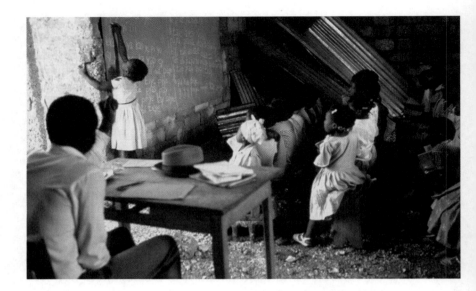

with basic human rights provide a consistent model. In this way a sports or mathematics teacher, for example, can also teach for human rights.

Dealing with difficult issues

Sometimes controversial and sensitive subjects come up when students begin to examine human rights. Teachers need to remain constantly alert to student discomfort and potential disagreement. Teachers should acknowledge that human rights necessarily involve conflicts of values and that students will benefit from understanding these conflicts and seeking to resolve them.

Sometimes teachers meet resistance to human rights education on the ground that it imposes non-native principles that contradict and threaten local values and customs. Teachers concerned about resistance from administrators should meet with them in advance, share goals and plans for the class, and explain about the United Nations human rights framework and related educational initiatives (such as the United Nations Decade for Human Rights Education). Encourage administrators to visit a class – they may themselves benefit from human rights education!

Pedagogical techniques for human rights education

The techniques suggested below and their application in the activities offered in Chapters Two and Three illustrate how teachers can engage students' empathy and moral imagination, challenge their assumptions and integrate concepts like human dignity and equality into their everyday experience of people, power and responsibility. These techniques have proved especially appropriate for human rights education because they encourage critical thinking, both cognitive and affective learning, respect for differences of experience and opinion, and active engagement of all participants in ongoing learning.

[A] Brainstorming

This technique can be used to seek solutions to problems that are both theoretical and practical. It requires a problem to be analysed and then solutions to be developed. Brainstorming encourages a high degree of participation, and it stimulates those involved to maximum creativity.

Following presentation of a problem, all ideas in response to it are recorded on a board or chart paper. All responses are recorded; no explanations are required and no suggestions are judged or rejected at this stage. The teacher then categorizes and analyses the responses, at which stage some are combined, adapted or rejected. Finally the group makes recommendations and takes decisions on the problem.

Examples: **"Message in a bottle" (p. 50); "Words that wound" (p. 64); "Identifying some 'minority groups'" (p. 73); "Housing" (p. 86); "Energy" (p. 88).**

[B] Case studies

Students in small groups work with real or fictional cases that require them to apply human rights standards. Case studies should be based on credible and realistic scenarios that focus on two or three main issues. The scenario for a study can be presented to students for consideration in its entirety or "fed" to them sequentially as a developing situation (the "evolving hypothetical") to which they must respond. This method encourages analysis, problem-solving and planning skills, as well as cooperation and team building. Case studies can be used to set up debates, discussion or further research.

Examples: **"A journalist has disappeared!" (p. 51); "Packing your suitcase" (p. 54); "When is 'old enough'?" (p. 65).**

© Creative expression

The arts can help to make concepts more concrete, personalize abstractions and affect attitudes by involving emotional as well as intellectual responses to human rights. Techniques may include stories and poetry, graphic arts, sculpture, drama, song and dance. Teachers do not need to be artists themselves but to set engaging tasks and provide a way for students to share their creations.

Examples: **"A 'Who am I?' book" (p. 35); "The lifeline" (p. 36); "Me on the wall/ground" (p. 36); "Letters and friends" (p. 39); "Wants and needs" (p. 45); "What does a child need?" (p. 46); "Promoting children's rights" (p. 46); "They're all alike" (p. 70).**

© Discussion

Many techniques exist for stimulating meaningful discussion in pairs, small groups or the whole class. To create an environment of trust and respect, students might develop their own "rules for discussion".

Discussions can be structured in a variety of effective ways. Some topics are appropriate to a formal debate, panel or *"Fish Bowl"* format (i.e. a small group discusses while the rest of the class listens and later makes comments and ask questions).

Other topics are better suited to a *"Talking Circle"* (i.e. students sit in two circles, one facing outward and the other inward. They discuss with the person sitting opposite; after a period the teachers asks everyone in the inside circle to move one place to the right and discuss the same topic with a new person). Personal or emotional topics are best discussed in pairs or small groups.

To engage the whole class in a topic, the teacher might use techniques like a *"Talk Around"* (i.e. the teacher asks an open-ended question like "What does dignity mean to you?" or "I feel happy when ..." and each student responds in turn).

A lively method of representing discussion graphically is the *"Discussion Web"*. Students sit in a discussion circle and speak one at a time. As they do, they pass a ball of yarn along, letting it unwind in the process. Each person keeps hold of the string whenever it passes through her or his hands. Eventually the group is linked by a web of string, clearly showing the pattern of communication that has gone on within it.

Examples: **"A circle for talking" (p. 35); "Me and my senses" (p. 37); "Wishingcircle" (p. 37); "Planning for a new country" (p. 43); "Being a human being" (p. 50); "Beginnings and endings" (p. 51); "Equality before the law" (p. 59); "The right to learn your rights" (p. 82).**

E Field trips/Community visits

Students benefit from the extension of school into the community, learning from places where human rights issues develop (e.g. courts, prisons, international borders) or where people work to defend rights or relieve victims (e.g. non-profit organizations, food or clothing banks, free clinics).

The purpose of the visit should be explained in advance, and students should be instructed to pay critical attention and to record their observations for a subsequent discussion or written reflection following the visit.

Examples: **"Councils and courts" (p. 57); "Who is not in our school?" (p. 80); "Food" (p. 84); "Health" (p. 88).**

F Interviews

Interviews provide direct learning and personalize issues and history. Those interviewed might be family and community members, activists, leaders or eye-witnesses to human rights events. Such oral histories can contribute to documenting and understanding human right issues in the home community.

Examples: **"Councils and courts" (p. 57); "Once upon a time" (p. 68); "Speakers on disability" (p. 79); "Speakers from the business community" (p. 93)**

G Research projects

Human rights topics provide many opportunities for independent investigation. This may be formal research using library or Internet facilities or informational research drawing on interviews, opinion surveys, media observations and other techniques of data gathering. Whether individual or group projects, research develops skills for independent thinking and data analysis and deepens understanding of the complexity of human rights issues.

Examples: **"Packing your suitcase" (p. 54); "Child soldiers" (p. 54); "Humanitarian law" (p. 55); "Councils and courts" (p. 57); "An International Criminal Court" (p. 61); "Identifying some 'minority groups'" (p. 73); "Food" (p. 84); "Work" (p. 87); "Energy" (p. 88).**

H Role-plays/Simulations

A role-play is like a little drama played out before the class. It is largely improvised and may be done as a story (with a narrator and key characters) or as a situation (where the key characters interact, making up dialogue on the spot - perhaps with the help of the teacher and the rest of the class). Role-plays have particular value for sensitizing students to the feelings and perspectives of other groups and to the importance of certain issues.

Role-plays work best when kept short. Allow enough time for discussion afterwards: it is crucial for children to be able to express themselves about feelings, fears or understandings after such activities, to maximize possible benefits and dissipate negative feelings, if any. Teachers may need to discourage students from becoming their role. Participants should be able to step back from what they are doing, to comment perhaps, or to ask questions. Other members of the class should be able to comment and question too, perhaps even joining in the role-play.

Variations on role-plays include mock trials, imaginary interviews, simulation games, hearings and tribunals. These usually have more structure, last longer and require more preparation of both teachers and students.

Examples: **"My puppet family" (p. 38); "Summit" (p. 53); "Councils and courts" (p. 57); "Sorts of courts" (p. 59); "Working life" (p. 90); "A model United Nations simulation" (p. 95).**

Visual aids

Learning can be enhanced by the use of blackboards, overhead transparencies, posters, displayed objects, flip charts, photographs, slides, videos and films. As a general rule, information produced on transparencies and charts should be brief and concise, and in outline or list form. If more text is required, use hand-outs. However, visual aids can be overused and should never substitute for engaged discussion and direct student participation.

Evaluation

Information content and levels of understanding of the students can be tested in standard ways. However, assessing attitudes and attitude change is much harder because of the subjective nature of the judgements involved. Open-ended questionnaires given at repeated intervals are the simplest, but the impressions they provide are fleeting at best.

It is equally difficult to evaluate whether the human rights climate of the school community has improved. However, if indicators for success are carefully defined and evaluation is done on a regular basis, changes in the school environment can be monitored and responded to.

Engaging students in drawing up checklists to assess individual, classroom and school community practices in human rights terms can be an important learning activity (see "Taking the Human Rights Temperature of Your School", p. 97).

Chapter Two

Human Rights Topics for Preschool and Lower Primary School

Confidence and social respect

In preschool and lower primary education, teaching for human rights is aimed at fostering feelings of confidence and respect for self and others. These are the basis for the whole culture of human rights. This makes the teacher's "teaching personality" highly important. A supportive approach at all times will make every activity meaningful, even those not specific to human rights teaching.

Stories are invaluable. Young children can learn lessons and morals and remember them vividly if they are associated with a much-loved character in a well-told tale. Such stories can be obtained from published literature on children's tales, from parents and grandparents or even by using one's imagination.

A classroom library where resources are available may be useful. In selecting books, it is important to obtain attractive volumes that feature both females and males as multicultural, active and non-stereotyped characters. When reading to the class or showing picture books, point out the good things they show or tell.

Where the resources exist, students can participate in cooking, a wood-work bench or potting plants. These can be done as imagination games also. All activities should involve both boys and girls. If disagreement arises concerning activities, the class may need to make rules to equalize the situation and break down discriminatory behaviour. Such rules become unnecessary with regular use. Equality can also be improved by changing the way the classroom is arranged or how students line up. It is important to avoid grouping children in ways that reinforce obvious differences. Try to facilitate friendships between students as well as awareness that differences are acceptable and natural.

Resolving conflicts

Conflicts often arise, and teachers need to develop a consistent strategy to address them. It is imperative that a teacher remain open to discussion of conflict at all times. Emphasize that a solution can be found to any problem. However, children need to think about a problem in order to find a solution. The following shows a more systematic approach to problem-solving:

1. Identify a problem and acknowledge it. Stop any physical or verbal activity and ask the children involved to discuss their behaviour together.
2. Get a description of what happened. Ask the children involved and any bystanders about the events that took place. Give everyone a turn to speak without interruption. Positive encouragement, such as a touch or a hug where appropriate, can also ease feelings of anger or guilt. However, it is essential to remain neutral at all times.
3. Explore a range of solutions. Ask those directly involved how this problem can be solved. If the children cannot suggest solutions, the teacher can offer some ideas.
4. Reason out the solutions. Point out how more than one fair solution may often exist. Encourage the children to think of the physical and emotional consequences of these solutions and recall past experiences of a similar nature.
5. Choose a course of action. Seek a mutual agreement on one of the solutions presented.
6. Carry out that action.

Confronting discrimination

In cases of discriminatory behaviour, solutions are not so easy to find. Usually neither the insulted child nor the offending child has a clear understanding of discrimination. The teacher's actions are especially important in this situation. The teacher should first strongly criticize the discriminatory behaviour and make clear that it is definitely unacceptable. The teacher may offer clear support to the child who was the object of the offence without criticism of his or her anger, fear or confusion, and be firm yet supportive with the child who engaged in the discriminatory behaviour. Teachers should help victimized children realize that negative responses to their gender, appearance, disability, language, race or other aspects are due to unacceptable prejudices; they should also examine with children who were involved and who witnessed the situation the issues at stake. Discuss such incidents also with parents, staff and members of the local community.

This method can be used at all school levels as well as in critical situations outside the school environment. It can be applied to all discriminatory behaviour. Where possible, ethnic diversity in the classroom should be acknowledged, understood and even celebrated at every opportunity. It should be remembered that racism and sexism are usually present in children at a very young age, so this method may be remedial. Teachers should also be aware that they too may harbour discriminatory attitudes and strive diligently to recognize and overcome them.

Care should also be taken to make the classroom and school accessible and welcoming to children with disabilities.

The following strategies and activities offer ways to introduce human rights concepts into early childhood education.

Appreciating similarities and differences

Attributes

Children are seated in a circle. One child stands in the middle of the circle and makes a statement that describes himself or herself. For example: "Is wearing a belt" or "Has a sister". Everyone who shares that attribute must change places, including the child in the middle. Whoever is left without a seat becomes the person in the middle and names the next attribute. Children will quickly see that they can be similar and different in many ways. An interesting ending would be to choose a more intangible attribute, such as: "People who are kind". The game usually breaks down at this point because it becomes more difficult to identify such attributes at a glance. Teachers may wish to discuss how people usually recognize such behavioral attributes.

(UDHR articles 1, 2; CRC article 2)

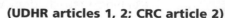

B In the same boat

The teacher explains that people sometimes don't recognize ways in which they are alike. Then the teacher names a category (e.g. month of birth, number of siblings, kind of pet, favourite toy or game) and asks children to form a group with others who share that category with them. Older children can respond to more complex categories (e.g. number of languages spoken, career aspiration, hobby, favourite school subject). The game concludes with the question "What did you learn from this activity?" and a discussion of people's unrecognized similarities and differences.

(UDHR article 2; CRC article 2)

Fostering confidence and self-esteem

1. Who am I and what am I like?

A A " Who Am I?" book

Children begin a book about themselves, with a self-portrait on the cover. Personal pictures, prose and poems can be collected in this book. As children learn to write, they can put personal details, questions about themselves and answers to questions in it too. If resources are limited, a book can be made for the whole class with a page or two for each child.

(UDHR articles 3, 19; CRC articles 6, 7, 8, 12, 13, 30)

B A circle for talking

Children sit in a circle that includes the teacher and any visitors. The teacher makes an open-ended statement and each student answers in turn. Questions might be one or more of the following:

– What I like best about myself is ...

– I'd like to be ...

– My favourite game is ...

– I think my name means ...

– I would like to learn about ...

– I feel happy when ...

– I feel sad when ...

– I want to become more ...

– Some day I hope ... .

Listening without interrupting and sharing time equally are very important. Children can "pass" if they do not wish to speak. Each person remains seated until the activity is over. Answers can be included in the "Who Am I?" book(s).

(UDHR articles 18, 19; CRC articles 8, 12, 13, 14, 17, 31)

C The lifeline

Each child stretches out a piece of yarn that represents his or her own life. Children then hang on their yarn drawings, stories and objects that convey the important things that have happened to them. This can be done in chronological sequence, or in any order that the child may want. It can also be extended into the future.

(UDHR articles 1, 3, 19; CRC articles 6, 8, 12, 13, 14, 27, 30, 31)

D Me on the wall/ground

Trace the outline of each child on a large piece of paper (best done lying down) or on the ground. Have the student draw/paint in physical details, and then write around personal and physical qualities (e.g. name, height, weight, what the child would most like to learn or do at school or in adulthood). If you have used papers, pin them up around the wall. Allow all students to learn about each other as well as themselves.

(UDHR articles 3, 19, 24; CRC articles 6, 7, 8, 12, 13, 28, 29, 31)

🄴 Me and my senses

Have children discuss in the circle, or use a role-play to explore the following statements:

– Hearing helps me to ...

– Seeing helps me to ...

– Smelling helps me to ...

– Touching helps me to ...

– Tasting helps me to ... .

Rephrase the questions, where appropriate, to suit the needs of children with disabilities (e.g. "Not being able to see (very well? at all?) I'm still me, and I can . . ."). Get each child to invent an instrument to help them hear, smell or touch better. Have them describe, draw or dramatize it.

(UDHR articles 22, 25, 26; CRC articles 23, 26, 28, 29)

🄵 Wishing-circle

Arrange the students in a circle. Propose that each child in turn makes the following wishes (this can also be done in small groups or pairs):

– If I could be any animal, I'd be _____ because ...

– If I could be a bird, I'd be _____ because ...

– If I could be an insect, I'd be _____ because ...

– If I could be a flower, I'd be _____ because ...

– If I could be a tree, I'd be _____ because ...

– If I could be a piece of furniture, I'd be _____ because ...

– If I could be a musical instrument, I'd be _____ because ...

– If I could be a building, I'd be _____ because ...

– If I could be a car, I'd be _____ because ...

– If I could be a street, I'd be _____ because ...

– If I could be a town/province/region, I'd be ____ because ...

– If I could be a foreign country, I'd be _____ because ...

– If I could be a game, I'd be _____ because ...

– If I could be a record, I'd be _____ because ...

– If I could be a TV show, I'd be _____ because ...

– If I could be a movie, I'd be _____ because ...

– If I could be a food, I'd be _____ because ...

– If I could be any colour, I'd be _____ because ... .

(UDHR article 19; CRC articles 13, 14)

2. How do I live with others?

[A] My puppet family

Each child makes a family of puppets that includes one of him or herself. These can be very simple, like cardboard cut-outs coloured and fixed to sticks or clay or mud figures. The figures are named and their relationships described and explained. Each child then devises a ceremony (a wedding, for example) or a festival, which is shown to the others in the class. The puppet family can be extended to include other people who live nearby. Children can dramatize something they do regularly with those people in order to bring them together. Extend the activity to include individuals from anywhere in the world.

**(UDHR articles 16, 20, 27;
CRC articles 9, 10, 15, 31)**

[B] Imaginary friend

The children sit or lie down quietly with their eyes closed. Tell them to breathe in deeply and then breathe out slowly. Repeat two more times. Now tell them to imagine a special place, a favourite place, anywhere in the world (or even in outer space). Say that they are walking in that place – in their imagination – feeling and hearing and seeing what is going on there. Lead them to a house or building they can visualize, where they go in to find a special room. The room has a door in one wall that opens by sliding up. The door slides up slowly, and as it does so, it reveals a special friend they have never met before – first feet, and finally the face. This friend can be old or young – anything. This friend is always there, and whenever they need someone to talk to, to turn to, they can visit him or her again if they wish. Close the door, leave the house and come home to the class. Let the children share what they have imagined in a speaking circle or in pairs or groups.

**(UDHR article 20;
CRC article 15)**

C Letters and friends

Set up a letter or electronic mail exchange with another class in another school or even another country. Initiate this exchange by sending poems or gifts from the class. This may lead to a visit later if the distance allows, and a chance to meet the children of the other community. Investigate the twin school:

- How big is it?
- What games are played there?
- What do the parents do?
- What are the differences and similarities?

(UDHR articles 19, 20, 26; CRC articles 13, 17, 29)

D Buddy

Teachers should arrange for their students to have an older buddy from an upper class. An activity should be arranged to encourage children to seek out the help of their buddy if they have a problem. Ways should be devised to encourage the senior buddy to take an interest in his or her small colleague by showing games and helping with activities.

(UDHR article 20; CRC article 15)

E People around me

Ask children in a talking circle to think of a good quality in themselves or ask "What are some qualities we admire in people?". Then lead a discussion on these topics:

- Do you respect in others the quality you like about yourself?
- Do you respect good qualities in others that you do not have?
- Do all human beings deserve respect? Why?
- How do you show respect for others?

Next ask children to think of a time when they felt hurt because someone did not respect them.

- How did disrespect feel?
- Why do people sometimes act disrespectfully to others?
- What is dignity? Is your dignity hurt when others do not respect you?
- What can you do when others do not respect you?

Finally,

- Ask "What does it mean if we say that all human beings deserve respect?"
- Ask for examples of how life in their community could be more peaceful if people showed greater respect for each other.
- Ask children to think of one way they could show respect for someone.

(UDHR articles 1, 2, 12; CRC articles 2, 12, 13, 14, 16, 29)

The washing machine

Have the children form two parallel lines close together, and facing each other. Send a child from one end between the lines ("through the wash"). Everyone (where this is culturally appropriate) pats him or her on the back or shakes his or her hand while offering words of praise, affection and encouragement. The result is a sparkling, shining, happy individual at the end of the "wash". He or she joins a line, and the process is then repeated for another child. (Running one or two people through daily is more fun than washing everybody in one big clean-up.)

(UDHR articles 1, 2; CRC article 2)

Building trust

Trust begins with teacher/student relationships. Putting students at ease involves:

- Letting the students know that the teacher is just as human as they are;
- Explaining each and every activity thoroughly;
- Explaining unfamiliar words and ideas (concepts);

• Providing information (not just about specific activities but also about relevant issues touching students' lives).

Where appropriate, the teacher should spend a few minutes of the day discussing local events and news items from the media. This will provide many opportunities to look at human rights issues in a less formal way. It can be an education in itself.

Blind trust

Divide the class into pairs. Have one child blindfold the other and have the sighted member of the pair lead the "blind" one about for a few minutes. Make sure the leading child is not abusing the power to lead, since the idea is to nurture trust, not to destroy it. The "leader" of the pair should try to provide as wide a variety of experiences as possible, such as having the "blind" partner feel things with his or her feet or fingers, leading with vocal directions or even playing a game.

After a few minutes have the children reverse the roles and repeat the process so that the "leader" is now the led, and the "blind" partner is now the sighted one.

Once the activity is over, allow the children to talk about what happened. Discuss how they felt – not just as "blind" partners but their feelings of responsibility as "leaders" too.

This can lead not only to a greater awareness of what life is like for people with sight (or hearing) disabilities, but to a discussion of the importance of trust in the whole community. This can lead in turn to a discussion of world society, how it works and how it can fail to work too.

(UDHR article 28; CRC articles 3, 23)

Creating classroom rules

The importance of classroom climate and the need for participation and cooperation cannot be emphasized enough. The children's suggestions and opinions are also very helpful in creating the best classroom atmosphere. Be open to their help and provide necessary changes.

The next activity is very significant because it has a direct effect on classroom climate. It clearly demonstrates a teacher's willingness to involve the class in how the classroom is run and her or his own trust in its members. It also makes children think about what rules are desirable and possible in class, how they might be observed and the teacher's own role in maintaining the classroom environment.

Ⓐ Classroom needs

Classroom rules can be created in a number of ways: as a brainstorm (paring down the results in subsequent discussion); in small groups that then present their findings to a plenary session of the whole class; or as individual assignments that the teacher collates for class consideration later.

A good way to begin is by asking children what they "want" (the list may become quite long). Then ask them to choose from this list the items they think are really needed. They should end up with something shorter and much more essential. List these on a chart labelled "Our Classroom Needs". Finally, ask them to choose from their "needs" what they think they have a "right" to expect as members of society. List these on a chart labelled "Our Classroom Rights". Ask why they have chosen as they have.

(UDHR articles 7, 21; CRC articles 12, 13, 28, 29)

Ⓑ Classroom responsibilities

Emphasize the essential connection between rights and responsibilities. After students have created the list of classroom rights, ask them to rephrase each right in terms of responsibilities and list these in a separate chart labelled "Our Classroom Responsibilities" (e.g. "Everyone should feel safe in this room" might be revised as "Everyone has the responsibility not to insult anybody or hurt anyone's feelings").

(UDHR article 29; CRC article 29)

Ⓒ Living with rights and responsibilities

Once the class has agreed on its lists of basic rights and responsibilities, display them so that they can be referred to or amended as necessary. Sometimes children or the teacher may break the rules or situations may arise that the rules do not address. Sometimes conflicts may arise when classroom rules are not compatible with the rules of other teachers or the school administration. These situations call for discussion and careful consideration of why things are going wrong. Order achieved by general consensus rather than simple control is always harder to get, and the process of reaching this consensus calls for compromise and careful negotiation. Such a process is itself a valuable learning experience.

(UDHR articles 7, 11, 21; CRC articles 12, 13, 28, 29)

Understanding human rights

Having arrived at some classroom rules, it is a natural next step to consider the same sort of thing on a universal scale.

[A] Planning for a new country

Explain that a new land has been discovered that has everything needed to sustain human life. No one has ever lived there before. There are no laws and no history. The whole class will be settling there. A small group has been appointed to draw up a list of rights for this all-new country. You do not know what position you will have in the new country.

Working in small groups, students in each group give this country a name and list ten rights the whole group can agree upon. Each group presents its list and the whole class makes a "class list" that includes all the rights mentioned. Discuss the class list (e.g. what would happen if some rights were excluded? Have any important rights been left out? How is this list different from your classroom rules?)

(UDHR articles 13, 21, 26; CRC articles 12, 13)

[B] Introducing the Universal Declaration of Human Rights

Introduce the Universal Declaration of Human Rights, explaining that it is a list of rights for all people in the world. Then read the simplified version aloud (see annex 1). If students hear an article that matches one of the rights on the class list, write the number of that article next to the right.

After completing the reading, discuss the results:

- Were any rights in the Universal Declaration left off the class list? Do students now want to add any new rights to the list?
- Were any rights on the class list left out of the Universal Declaration?
- Does the Universal Declaration include responsibilities as well as rights?

Students might try similar exercises using a simplified version of the Convention on the Rights of the Child.

(UDHR articles 21, 26; CRC article 29)

Introducing children's rights

[A] What are children's rights?

Ask students whether there are rights and responsibilities that apply more specifically to them, not just as people but as young people – as children. What might it be wrong to do (or not to do) to someone just because he or she happens, at that point in time, to be "a child"?

Introduce the Convention on the Rights of the Child, explaining that it guarantees to children the things they need to grow up healthy, safe and happy and to become good citizens in their community. Help children understand the relationship between needs and rights.

Discuss:

- Why do you think the United Nations has adopted a document just for children's human rights? How are children's needs different from those of adults?
- Why do children need special protection? Give some examples?
- Why do children need special provisions for their welfare. What do children need for their survival, happiness and development?

- Why do children need to participate in their communities? Give some examples.
- Who is responsible for seeing that children's rights are respected? (e.g. parents? teachers? other adults? other children? the Government?)

B Wants and needs

Ask children working in small groups to create ten cards that illustrate things that children need to be happy. They can cut pictures from old magazines or draw these things. Help them label the cards. Each group explains and posts its cards under the heading "Needs".

Next announce that the new Government has found that it can only provide some of the items on the list, so the group must eliminate ten items from the list of needs. Remove the cards selected and post them under the heading "Wants".

Then announce that still further cuts are required and the group must eliminate another ten items and follow the same procedure.

Finally discuss this activity:

- What items were eliminated first? Why?
- What is the difference between wants and needs?
- Do wants and needs differ for different people?
- What would happen if the class had to go on eliminating needs?

Conclude by explaining that children's rights are based on what all children need to live a healthy, happy life and grow up to be responsible citizens. Introduce the Convention on the Rights of the Child as an effort to make sure that all children have these rights (see activity "What are children's rights?" above). Older children might read aloud the summarized version of the Convention (see annex 2) and compare it to their list of wants and needs.[8]

---

[8] Adapted from *It's Only Right! A Practical Guide to Leaning about the Convention on the Rights of the Child* by Susan Fountain (UNICEF, 1993).

C. What does a child need?

Working in small groups, students draw a large outline of a child (or outline one of them) and give the child a name.  They then decide on the mental, physical, spiritual and character qualities they want this ideal child to have as an adult (e.g. good health, sense of humour, kindness) and write these qualities inside the outline. They might also make symbols on or around the child to represent these ideal qualities (e.g. books to represent education). Outside the child, the group lists the human and material resources the child will need to achieve these qualities (e.g. if the child is to be healthy, it will need food and health care). Each group then "introduces" its new member of the community and explains its choices for the child.

Introduce the Convention on the Rights of the Child (see activity "What are children's rights?" above). Then read aloud the summarized version of the Convention (see annex 2). When children hear an article that guarantees a child each of the needs they have listed, they write the number of the article(s) next to that item. Circle any needs identified by the class but not covered by the Convention.

D. Promoting children' s rights

In some countries children's rights are advertised by newspapers, radio and television. Ask students working in small groups to make up some advertisements for particular articles of the Convention on the Rights of the Child (e.g. posters, skits, songs or other forms). Ask each group to perform or exhibit their ideas for the class as a whole.

Chapter Three

Human Rights Topics for Upper Primary and Lower and Senior Secondary School

A human rights culture attempts to define principles for the positive conduct of all human behaviour. What follows are issues involved in realizing these principles. Although only a few activities are described for each issue, they should provide teachers with a start for developing their own activities. As some of these issues may prove to be controversial, the teacher's sensitivity and discretion are required.

Teachers who want to concentrate on specific issues (e.g. peace and disarmament, world development, prisoners of conscience, minority peoples, anti-racism or anti-sexism) should present them in a human rights context. Students will then be able to see that what they discuss is only one aspect of a larger framework involving many other issues. This general understanding will provide breadth while the specific issue will provide depth. Teachers who specialize in different aspects of human rights should work side by side to provide understanding in depth.

Protecting life – the individual in society

To establish a clear sense of humanity as a composite of individuals, the teacher can explore with students the concept of what being "human" means. This is a more sophisticated form of the activities in Chapter Two on confidence and respect. Human beings are social creatures; we have individual personalities, but we learn most things by living with others. Hence work about the individual is work about society too.

🄰 Being a human being

Place a convenient object (e.g. an inverted wastepaper bin) before the class. Suggest that it is a visitor from another part of the universe. This visitor is curious to learn about the beings who call themselves "human". Ask for suggestions that might help the visitor identify us as "human beings".

Discuss:
• What does it mean to be "human"?
• How is that different from just being alive or "surviving"?

(UDHR article 1; CRC article 1)

🄱 Message in a bottle

Ask students to imagine that signals have been received from outer space. The United Nations is going to send information about human beings in a special ship. It is the students' job to choose what to send (e.g. music, models of people, clothing, literature, religious objects). Brainstorm possibilities as a class, or set the activity as an individual or small group project.

The questions at issue here – "What am I?", "Who are we?" – are profound. The activities above should provide an opportunity for students to begin to establish a sense of themselves as human beings and an understanding of human dignity. This is crucial if they are ever to see themselves as human agents, with a responsibility to humanity in all its many and varied forms. Defining what is human in general helps us to see what might be inhuman.

(UDHR article 1; CRC article 1)

Ⓒ Beginnings and endings

Human beings within societies are of the highest complexity. At the teacher's discretion, the class can look at the right to be alive as argued for at each end of an individual's life:
* Where does "life" begin?
* Could it ever be taken away?
* What kind of factors determine our opinions about what "life" means (e.g. religion, technology, law)?

(UDHR article 3; CRC article 6)

Ⓓ " A journalist has disappeared!"

For the following case study the teacher's discretion is advised. Provide the class with the following details:

You are a journalist. You wrote a story in your newspaper that made someone in a high position angry. The next day unidentified people broke into your home and took you away. You were beaten and put in a room alone. No one knows where you are. No one has offered to do anything. You have been there for months.

This journalist has been deprived of a number of basic rights. Using the Universal Declaration, ask the class to determine which specific articles have been violated.

Ask each student to draft a letter to the Minister of Justice concerned, mentioning these rights, or an open letter to the journalist. Who else could be of assistance in this case (introducing students to the role of civil society's organizations)?

(UDHR articles 3, 5, 8, 9, 11, 12)

Ⓔ Protecting children

Look through the Convention on the Rights of the Child and list all the articles that offer protection to children and the circumstances and specific forms of abuse and exploitation that these articles mention.

- Are there others that you might add?
- Are some children more vulnerable and in need of protection than others?

Discuss responsibility for protecting children:
- According to the Convention, who has the responsibility for protecting children?
- Does the Convention give any order of priority for this responsibility?
- What happens when those responsible for protecting children fail to do so?

Research child protection in your community, using the list generated at the beginning of this activity.
- What are children's particular needs for protection in your community?
- What people or groups are providing protection for them?
- Are there ways you and your class can contribute to this protection?
- Why do you think that the rights of children needed to be expressed in a special human rights treaty?

(CRC articles 2, 3, 6, 8, 11, 16, 17, 19, 20, 22, 23, 32, 33, 34, 35, 36, 37, 38)

War, peace and human rights

The Universal Declaration of Human Rights (UDHR) was written in response to the devastating events of the Second World War. In the preamble, the Declaration states that "disregard and contempt for human rights have resulted in barbarous acts which have outraged the conscience of mankind" and stresses that "recognition of the inherent dignity and of the equal and inalienable rights of all members of the human family is the foundation of freedom, justice and peace in the world".

Peace, disarmament, development and human rights are interrelated issues. A comprehensive approach to teaching for human rights is teaching for peace and disarmament, as well as for development and environmental awareness.

Information on the arms race and on the attempts to control it could be provided to students. The fact that there have been more than 150 conflicts since the end of the Second World War shows that armed violence continues to be used. Depending on the level of the class, a study of international political and economic issues would also deepen students' understanding of why peace is so hard to preserve. Developmental imbalances and ecological problems are also endemic; they are not only violent in themselves, but may contribute to sowing the seeds of war. And war – in particular nuclear war – even on a small scale, can result in an environmental catastrophe.

Ⓐ Peace

Pick a fine day if possible. Pose the question: "In a world with local conflicts and the threat of war, why do you think peace is important?"

Take the class outside, perhaps, to somewhere pleasant. Everybody lies on their backs without talking and shuts their eyes for approximately three minutes. Resume the class and discuss the fundamental value of peace. How would they define "peace"? What is the relationship between peace and human rights?

(UDHR articles 1, 3, 28; CRC articles 3, 6)

Ⓑ Summit

Role-play a summit discussion between the leaders of all countries about a critical issue, for example reduction in the use of land mines or the protection of children from dangerous work. Stage a classroom debate on the topic, with groups working together as the countries involved: some groups trying to ban these practices, some groups refusing to ban. Compare, when feasible, the discussions that led to the Convention on the Prohibition of Anti-Personnel Mines (1997) or the Convention concerning the Prohibition of the Worst Forms of Child Labour (International Labour Organization's Convention No. 182, 1999). Emphasize that different countries and people can work together in ways that allow all of us to live together in peace. (See the activity *A model United Nations simulation* below for an alternative format.)

(UDHR article 28; CRC articles 3, 4, 6(c))

C Packing your suitcase

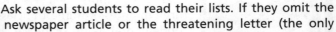

One of the common results of war and oppression is the creation of refugees, people who flee their home countries because of a "well-founded fear of persecution for reasons of race, religion, nationality, membership in a particular social group or political opinion" (article 1.A.2 of the Convention relating to the Status of Refugees, 1951).

Read this scenario:

You are a teacher in _____. Your partner disappears and is later found murdered. Your name appears in a newspaper article listing suspected subversives. Later you receive a letter threatening your life because of your alleged political activities. You decide you must flee. Pack your bag. You can take only five categories of things (e.g. toiletries, clothing, photographs) and only what you can carry in one bag by yourself. You have five minutes to make these decisions. Remember that you may never return to your home country again.

Ask several students to read their lists. If they omit the newspaper article or the threatening letter (the only concrete proof to offer authorities in the new country that they are fleeing a "well-grounded fear of persecution"), say "Asylum denied". After a few such examples, explain the definition of a refugee and the importance of proof of persecution. Discuss the experience of making emotional decisions in a state of anxiety.

Research refugees in the world today:

- Where are the greatest concentrations of refugees?
- Where are they fleeing from and why?
- Who is responsible for caring for them?

(UDHR article 14; CRC article 22)

D Child soldiers

In some parts of the world, boys and girls, even younger than ten years old, are recruited to serve as soldiers. Often these children are kidnapped and forced into this dangerous work, which can lead to death, maiming and alienation from their home communities and society as a whole. A new Optional Protocol (2000) to the Convention on the Rights of the Child bans the involvement of children in such armed conflict, as does the International Labour Organization's Convention concerning the Prohibition of the Worst Forms of Child Labour (1999).

Discuss:

- Why would armed forces want to use children in warfare?
- What human rights of these children are being violated? Cite particular articles of the Convention on the Rights of the Child.
- How might being a child soldier affect girls and boys differently?
- If a child manages to survive and return to the home community, what are some difficulties that she or he might face at first? In the short term? In the long term?

Here are some ways in which students can take action or explore the issue further:

- Find out more about child soldiers in different parts of the world;
- Find out what organizations are working to rehabilitate former child soldiers and offer them support;
- Write letters encouraging the Government to ratify the Optional Protocol to the Convention on the Rights of the Child banning the involvement of children in armed conflict.

(UDHR articles 3, 4, 5;
CRC articles 3, 6, 9, 11, 32, 34, 36, 37, 38, 39)

📖 Humanitarian law

Operating parallel to international human rights law is the complementary legal system of international humanitarian law. Embodied in the Geneva Conventions of 1949, these so-called "rules of war" establish standards for the protection of wounded, sick and shipwrecked military personnel, prisoners of war and civilians living in war zones or under enemy occupation. Military forces in many countries train their personnel in the Geneva Conventions, and the International Committee of the Red Cross (ICRC) takes a global lead in educating the public in international humanitarian law as well as in supplying humanitarian relief during armed conflicts.

However, the reality of modern warfare has changed. The combatants are no longer just the armies of warring countries (international armed conflict) but also rebel armies, terrorists or competing political or ethnic groups (non-international armed conflict). Furthermore, most victims are no longer soldiers but civilians, especially women, children and the elderly.

In many ways, the human rights framework and international humanitarian law reinforce each other. For example, both show particular concern for children recruited as soldiers and recognize the need for special protection for children in situations of armed conflict.

Find out more about how human rights and humanitarian law apply in conditions of warfare:

- Research the history of the International Red Cross and Red Crescent Movement and the Geneva Conventions. How have the original Geneva Conventions of 1949 been adapted to address the conditions of modern warfare?
- Find out about the humanitarian work of the International Committee of the Red Cross for victims of war. Compare the ICRC's seven fundamental principles (humanity, impartiality, neutrality, independence, voluntary service, unity and universality) with the principles of the Universal Declaration.
- Compare the provisions for children in war situations in the Convention on the Rights of the Child, the 1949 Fourth Geneva Convention (the Geneva Convention relative to the Protection of Civilian Persons in Time of War) and the 1977 Additional Protocols to the Geneva Conventions. Why are both international human rights law and international humanitarian law needed to protect children?
- Compare the Optional Protocol to the Convention on the Rights of the Child regarding the involvement of children in armed conflict and article 77 of Additional Protocol I to the Geneva Conventions regarding the recruitment of children. Which is more effective? Are both needed? Do you agree that a person of fifteen is old enough to serve as a soldier?
- Examine news reports of armed conflicts in the world today. Are the Geneva Conventions being observed in this conflict? Is the UDHR being observed?

**(UDHR articles 5, 9, 10, 11, 12, 13, 14, 21;
CRC articles 3, 6, 22, 30, 38, 39)**

Government and the law

Human rights are rights inherent in every human being. We can make moral claims regardless of whether they are laid down by law. For example, all human beings have a right to life, whether or not a law has been passed to endorse that right.

Laws, however, give moral claims legal force. In countries where rights have been made into laws, we still need to know whether these laws are being fully put into practice. Yet, turning moral claims into legal rights is an important first step.

Laws can also have an important educational effect. They define what a society officially thinks it is proper to do, and they provide a specific expression of the standards it thinks should be endorsed. They are there for all to see, and they stand equally – in principle at least – above the leaders as well as the led.

⒜ Councils and courts

Laws are made by national law-making bodies. Students need to see the process of law-making for themselves in order to answer these questions:
- What is "the law"?
- Who makes it? and
- Why?

Arrange for a class visit to a regional or central chamber of the country's parliament in session so that students can watch its members at work. Discuss the three questions above. Likewise, arrange a visit to a law-court to see not only laws being administered but also decisions being made that set legal precedents which may directly or indirectly affect future decisions. Discuss the same questions above.

If the suggested visits are not possible, or even if they are, organize the class into a model parliament and arrange a debate on current issues or a mock trial to adjudicate a local or national case at law. Encourage students to find suitable examples themselves.

To introduce an international dimension, teachers could have the class research the decision-making processes of the United Nations and the issues currently discussed. They could also review some cases brought before international commissions, tribunals and courts. (See the activity *An International Criminal Court* below.)

You may also wish to invite a local political figure to talk to the class about the three questions raised at the beginning of this activity, plus three more:
- Why are laws obeyed?
- How is "justice" done? And
- How is "fairness" achieved in government and the law?

Examine article 12 of the Convention on the Rights of the Child, which gives children the right to an opinion in matters that affect them. Has this right been recognized in the courts of your country? How?

Discuss:
- Are women given equal status before the law?
- How many women are lawyers in your country? Magistrates? Judges? Lawmakers in local or national legislative bodies?
- How do these numbers affect the way women are treated in law? (See the activities *Equality before the law and Making decisions* below.)

(UDHR articles 7, 8, 10, 12, 21, 40; CRC articles 12, 40)

🅱 Sorts of courts

Legislative processes can also be learned by arranging the class into an informal court. The "disputants" can be in the middle, with their "friends" and "family" close by and the rest of the class in a circle around them as a "village". Appoint a "magistrate" outside the circle as someone to be turned to only when the locals want an outsider's opinion. Have the disputants put their cases in turn, allowing everybody to elaborate their points. The discussion should continue until a consensus verdict is reached.

The issue to be dealt with can be chosen by the teacher with the students' help. Discuss afterwards how the "law" has worked here in both the formal and the informal cases. Note how it may be impossible to find someone to blame, particularly when each party has reasonable points to make.

(UDHR articles 8, 10; CRC articles 3, 12)

🅲 Equality before the law

Article 7 of the Universal Declaration begins: "All are equal before the law ...". However, this statement of principle is not always reflected in practice.

Discuss:
- Are all equal before the law in your community, or are some people treated in different ways?
- What factors might give some people an advantage over others?
- Why is equality before the law essential for a human rights culture?

(UDHR article 7; CRC article 2)

🅳 Comparing " rights" documents[9]

Point out that rights are guaranteed not only by international documents like the Universal Declaration (UDHR) but also by regional, national and local law codes such as nation-

---

[9] Adapted from *Teaching Human Rights* by David Shiman (Center for Teaching International Relations Publications, University of Denver, 1998).

al constitutions. Give students copies of the UDHR and any two other documents and ask them to compare whether each contains the following rights and to identify the relevant article(s):

1. Right to education
2. Freedom of expression (including the media)
3. Free choice of spouse
4. Equality of all persons, including women and minorities
5. Free choice of number of children
6. Freedom from torture and inhumane treatment
7. Freedom of thought, conscience and religion
8. Right to own property
9. Right to own firearms
10. Adequate food
11. Adequate shelter
12. Adequate health care
13. Right to travel freely within and outside the country
14. Right to peaceful assembly
15. Right to clean air and water

Discuss:

- What similarities and differences did you discover? How can you explain these?
- Does your Constitution or local law include more or fewer rights than the UDHR?
- Did the writers of these documents seem to have the same concept of what "rights" mean?
- Do all documents contain responsibilities as well as rights?
- Do citizens of your country have any rights besides those included in your Constitution or local law?
- What happens when these laws conflict?
- What should be the limits and responsibilities of Governments in guaranteeing their citizens certain rights? For example, is hunger or homelessness a Government's responsibility?
- Should any of the rights listed be guaranteed by all Governments?

(UDHR articles: all)

🎲 An International Criminal Court

At the international military trials held in 1945-1946 in Nuremberg and Tokyo, the victorious Allies prosecuted individual German and Japanese officials for "crimes against peace", "war crimes" and "crimes against humanity" committed in connection with the Second World War.

Since that time, such crimes and massive human rights violations have been committed in many other armed conflicts. In Cambodia, the Khmer Rouge killed an estimated 2 million people during the 1970s. Thousands of civilians, including horrifying numbers of unarmed women and children, lost their lives in armed conflicts in Mozambique, Liberia, El Salvador and other countries. However, international agreement to establish international courts to deal with such atrocities could not be reached until the 1990s, when the conflict in the former Yugoslavia erupted and war crimes, crimes against humanity and genocide – in the guise of "ethnic cleansing" – once again commanded international attention. In 1993, the United Nations Security Council established the ad hoc International Criminal Tribunal for the former Yugoslavia, to prosecute and punish individuals for those systematic and massive human rights violations. Similarly, following the end of the civil war that raged in Rwanda from April to July 1994, in which some 1 million unarmed civilians were massacred, the Security Council established the International Criminal Tribunal for Rwanda.

History has shown that without the enforcement mechanism of an international criminal court to deal with individual responsibility, acts of genocide and egregious human rights violations often go unpunished. Such a court could provide a complementary means by which to ensure that individuals can be prosecuted for genocide, war crimes and crimes against humanity when the country in which such crimes are perpetrated is unable or unwilling to prosecute. Also, such an institution could deter grave crimes under international law from being perpetrated in future. Accordingly, in 1998 government representatives met at a diplomatic conference in Rome to formulate a statute for a permanent international criminal court. On 17 July 1998, the Statute of the International Criminal Court was adopted: 120 Governments voted in favour, 7 against and 21 abstained. The Statute entered into force in July 2002, having been ratified by at least 60 States, and the International Criminal Court has now been set up in The Hague (Netherlands).

The establishment of the International Criminal Court raises several important issues and provides opportunities for student research and activity:

- Why is such a Court needed? Can it be effective?
- By what authority can the international community intervene in a country's internal matters, such as how a Government treats its own citizens? Is this interference in domestic affairs? (A class activity could be developed to discuss whether and when an international body has the right to intervene in a country's domestic affairs.)
- Find out more about the International Criminal Court (e.g. its rules of procedure, the kind of cases it will deal with, etc. – the official web site of the Court is http://www.icc.org). What will be the obligations of each Government to cooperate with the International Criminal Court?
- For the International Criminal Court to be set up, its Statute had to be ratified by at least 60 countries. Find out which countries have ratified it so far. If your own country has not yet ratified, hold a debate about the pros and cons of ratification. Send letters or petitions to your country's legislators urging your position(s) on ratification.
- Survey world history for examples of situations that might have been taken to an international criminal court, if such a court had existed at the time.

(UDHR articles 7, 10, 11, 28; CRC articles 3, 40, 41)

Freedom of thought, conscience, religion, opinion and expression

Freedom of thought, conscience, religion, opinion and expression is central to a human rights culture. The Convention on the Rights of the Child gives these rights to children based on their developing maturity (see activities *Growing maturity* and *When is old enough?* below). These rights include the freedom to change religion or belief; to hold opinions without interference; and to seek, receive and impart information and ideas through any media and regardless of frontiers.

Ⓐ Frames of reference

Opinions may vary depending on whether we like what we see or not. This is reflected in our choice of words. For example, a person can be described as "aloof" or "independent", "aggressive" or "assertive", "submissive" or "prepared to cooperate", "more driven" or "less afraid of hard work". Ask students to think of other dichotomies of this sort.

Have students list in the most positive way possible five qualities about themselves they really admire. Then put these into a negative frame of reference so that the same things become hurtful instead of praiseworthy. Then do the reverse, first listing possible negative qualities they do not particularly like about themselves, and then using mirror words that make the list less offensive.

Another version of this activity is to ask students to list adjectives that generally describe girls or boys. Then reverse the gender (e.g. qualities described as "energetic" or "ambitious" in a boy might be considered "abrasive" or "pushy" in a girl).

(UDHR articles 1, 2; CRC article 2)

🅱 Words that wound

Article 13.2.a of the Convention on the Rights of the Child gives a child the right to freedom of expression but specifically restricts expression that violates the rights and reputations of others. Should limits be placed on what we can say about our thoughts and beliefs? Should we always be able to say whatever we like? For the following activity the teacher's discretion is advised.

Give everyone slips of paper and have them write down hurtful comments they hear at school, each on a separate paper. Make a scale on the wall ranging from "Teasing/Playful" to "Extremely Painful/Degrading". Ask students to put their words where they think they belong on the scale (alternatively, papers can be collected and read by the teacher in order to ensure that inputs remain anonymous – students would then put them on the scale). Then ask everyone to examine the wall silently. Usually the same words will appear several times and almost always be rated at different degrees of severity.

Discuss this experience: ask students to categorize the words (e.g. appearance, ability, ethnic background, sexuality).

- Are some words only for girls? For boys?
- What conclusions can be drawn about abusive language from these categories?
- Why did some people think a particular word was very painful and others find it playful?

Divide the class into small groups and give each group several of the words considered most painful. Ask someone in each group to read the first word or phrase. The group should accept that this is a hurtful comment and discuss (1) whether people should be allowed to say such things (2) what to do when it happens. Repeat for each word or phrase.

Finally discuss with the class the rights and responsibilities involved in abusive language.

- Does a teacher have a responsibility to stop hate speech at school?
- Do students have a responsibility to stop it in their own lives? If so, why?
- What can you do in your community to stop hate speech?
- Why is it important to do so?

(UDHR articles 1, 2, 18, 19; CRC articles 12, 13, 14, 16, 17, 29)

Ⓒ Growing maturity

The Convention on the Rights of the Child gives children the right to freedom of thought, conscience and religion, according to their growing maturity. Ask students to debate when a young person is sufficiently mature to practice a religion or hold political views that differ from those of the family, culture or tradition. Who should decide?

(CRC article 14)

The right to privacy

Article 16 of the Convention on the Rights of the Child gives a child the right to protection from interference with privacy, family, home and correspondence and from libel or slander. However, like many other rights guaranteed to children in the Convention, the extent to which it can be exercised depends on the child's "evolving capacity". Certainly a seven-year-old is not ready to have the same rights and responsibilities as a seventeen-year-old.

When is " old enough" ?

Read the following story to the class:
Eku and Romit met when they sat side by side at primary school. They soon became best friends, but their friendship had a problem. Their families belonged to different social

groups that had a long history of distrust. So when Romit asked if Eku could visit, both parents firmly refused. Eku's family spoke to the teacher and had the friends seated separately. However, their friendship continued until Eku was sent away to finish secondary school in another town. The friends promised to write, but whenever a letter from Eku arrived, Romit's parents destroyed it before Romit could even open it. Romit understands his parents' feelings but also thinks that at sixteen you are old enough to choose your own friends and entitled to have letters kept private.

Discuss:

- What rights does Romit have according to the Convention on the Rights of the Child?
- How can Romit's "evolving capacity" be determined?
- What rights do Romit's parents have?

Strategize how this conflict might be resolved.

(UDHR article 12; CRC articles 5, 16)

The freedom to meet and take part in public affairs

How does a community maintain itself and flourish? In part, by having its members meet together and organize their affairs. These freedoms make communal involvement very important. Their denial would deprive a society of one of its richest resources: the skills and talents of its own people.

Habits of communal participation can be fostered throughout a student's schooling. Opportunities for community service outside the school can also become the basis for a lifelong contribution to social and political affairs. Many schools have student councils that allow participation in their affairs, though the adult hierarchy usually limits what can be done in practice.

A human rights club

A direct experience of working together for something worthwhile may be achieved from having the class form a club to promote human rights. The teacher can initiate a number of relevant tasks aimed at establishing such a club:

- Define the purpose of the Human Rights Club in more detail;
- Hold a competition for a club symbol;
- Make individual membership cards that carry this logo;
- Organize office-holders;
- Put up a special noticeboard for Human Rights Club activities;
- Find out about national and international human rights networks and organizations with which the club can liaise; ask for their publications and display these where people can use them;
- Begin holding meetings – the first could discuss the right to freedom of association itself: "Why organize? Why it is important to take part in public affairs, locally, nationally and beyond?"
- Invite guest speakers (e.g. local politicians, issue specialists, area specialists) to give short talks and hold discussions;
- Set up sub-committees to meet and to research particular tasks;
- Commemorate International Human Rights Day, 10 December; find out about other International Days related to human rights and commemorate them.[10]

A group could approach other classes with offers to speak to them about particular human rights issues/areas, explaining why the club was formed and what it does, and offering associate membership; where resources permit, the club could also publish a regular newsletter.

(UDHR articles 20, 21; CRC article 15)

---

[10] For practical ideas, see "*More than 50 Ideas for Commemorating the Universal Declaration of Human Rights*", available at http://www.ohchr.org or through the Office of the United Nations High Commissioner for Human Rights. A list of International Days is also available on the web site or through the Office.

Social and cultural well-being

The Universal Declaration and the Convention on the Rights of the Child provide for people to rest, learn, worship as they choose, share freely in the cultural life of the community and develop their personalities to the full. Schools should give students access to the arts and sciences of their region and the world and foster respect for the child's cultural identity, language and values, as well as those of others. They should also teach human rights issues using multicultural examples from different historical periods.

Much of a sense of personal and social well-being is derived from the family. Families take the form most relevant to the culture and economy in which its members live, ranging from single-adult units in separate enclaves to extended kinship systems that embrace whole communities. Article 18 of the Convention on the Rights of the Child recognizes the joint primary responsibility of both parents for bringing up their children and article 20 provides for special protection for children without families, either in an alternative family or in an institution.

Most activities in the school curriculum are relevant to this topic. Discussions could perhaps begin with the process of education itself. Education (as opposed to schooling) is a lifelong affair and a truly comprehensive one, since every generation's culture must be learned again if it is not to disappear. (See also the activity *Cultural identity* below.)

⒜ Once upon a time ...

Invite a few grandparents to come and talk to the students about what they were taught as children and whether it served them well in later life. What rights now guaranteed by the Convention on the Rights of the Child did they lack in their childhood?

Ask them how they would foster the full development of the human personality, what they have learned about strengthening respect for human rights and freedoms, how they would further understanding and mutual respect between different human groups and nations and what makes for justice and peace.

(UDHR articles 19, 27; CRC articles 29, 31)

⬚ A family map

Have students map their family as it stands at the moment (teachers should be sensitive to the possibility of adoption cases in their classroom). Compare and discuss eventual differences:

How is their family life different from that of their great-grandparents? Their grandparents? Their parents?

What has caused these changes? Are they changes in values, culture, technology or others kinds of change? Which are beneficial and which are not?

Have the human rights of family members improved over the last generations?

(UDHR articles 16, 19, 27; CRC articles 5, 29, 31)

Discrimination

No person is more of a human being than another and no person is less. Essentially we are all equal, and equally entitled to our human rights.

Equal, yes, but not identical – a fact that leads people to draw lines across the human map and to draw attention to differences they believe to be important. When lines are established that not only separate groups but suggest that one group is superior or inferior simply because of race, colour, sex, language, religion, political opinion or national or social origin, this is discrimination.

Gender is among the most common bases for discrimination. Since it coincides with a biological dichotomy built into our species itself, it can be very hard for people to see past such a difference to our deeper identity. Being different in some ways does not make us different in all ways. Having different bodies that do different things does not mean that our human rights should be different too.

Another pernicious form of discrimination is colour or race. A particular difference is repeatedly over-emphasized to hide our common humanity.

No teacher can avoid the issue of discrimination. Human equality, and the life-chances and life-choices it promotes, does not just happen. It has to be taught, not least by exploring stereotyped attitudes and prejudices, by helping students to understand that they can be competent and caring, and by providing appropriate and accurate information.

This is a process of questioning that never ends. It is important to be informed about socio-economic and political issues and how they work. However, it is even more important for teachers to be aware of the biases and discriminatory attitudes that they themselves, like all people, harbour. The individual teacher bears a heavy personal responsibility of self-examination, for unless prejudices are recognized, they will persist and influence a generation of young people.

1. Discrimination – stereotypes

In confronting stereotypes, point out the danger of encouraging their opposite. Insist that any grain of truth there may be in a stereotype is just that – a grain. Alternatively, ask the class about occasions on which they may have heard such expressions as "They're all alike, aren't they" or "That lot are all the same".

They' re all alike

Give each student a small stone or some other ordinary object, such as a potato, and ask them to become "friends" with it – really get to know it. Ask a few to introduce their "friend" to the class, and to tell a story about how old it is, whether it is sad or happy, or how it got its shape. They can write essays on the subject, songs or poems of praise. Then put all the items back in a box or bag and mix them up together. Tip them out and have the students find their "friend" from among the common lot.

Point out the obvious parallel: any group of people seem to be alike at first, but once you get to know them, they are all different, they all have life-histories and they are potentially all friends. This means, however, suspending any stereotypes (like "rocks are cold and hard and indifferent") long enough to get to know them. It means not prejudging them.

(UDHR articles 1, 2; CRC article 2)

Spot the difference

Present the following statements:

1. I like doctors because they are always kind.
2. I like the fact that some doctors are kind to me.
3. Doctors are a kind lot.

Discuss which is the stereotype (No. 3), which is the prejudice (No. 1), and which is merely the statement of opinion (No. 2). Point out how all three statements (as mental frames of reference) will make it harder to appreciate doctors not only as kind and caring people, but as cross and impatient ones too! Discuss how stereotype, prejudice and opinion predetermine attitudes.

(UDHR article 2; CRC article 2)

2. Discrimination – colour or race

Racism is the belief that there are human groups with particular (usually physical) characteristics that make them superior or inferior to others. Racist behaviour can be not just overt, such as treating some people according to their race or colour, but also covert, when society systematically treats groups according to some form of discriminating judgement.

Racist behaviour often results in racial discrimination, with its obvious negative consequences, ranging from simple neglect, or the avoidance of those believed to be different and inferior, to more explicit forms of harassment, exploitation or exclusion.

A good source to examine is the International Convention on the Elimination of All Forms of Racial Discrimination (ICERD).

Skin colour is one of the most arbitrary ways of discriminating between people that humankind has ever devised. As an exercise, ask students to plan a multiracial society where they are destined to live, without knowing in advance what their own skin colour will be.

The non-racist classroom

There are many ways of making the classroom a place of acceptance and of multiracial celebration. Cultural factors influence a student's responses, such as how much eye contact he or she finds comfortable, how receptive he or she is to group learning strategies, or his or her style of dramatic play or story-telling. If and when there is a racial conflict in the class, deal with it; do not dismiss it. Teach your students how to recognize behaviour that may reinforce racism. Study the stories of famous people who have fought against discrimination. Study the contributions made by people from all parts of the world to the common stock of human knowledge and experience. Introduce as much cultural diversity as possible into the curriculum. Ask parents or other relatives or friends to help in this regard. Invite people of other races or colours who are active in community work to speak to the class about what they do.

(UDHR articles 1, 2; CRC article 2)

3. Discrimination – minority group status

The concept of a "minority group" is confused with the concepts of "ethnicity" and often "race", and when it is, earlier activities are relevant here as well. The term is a loose one, and has also been used to describe indigenous peoples, displaced peoples, migrant workers, refugees and even oppressed majorities. Often common to these groups is poverty. A minority group may cease to be a "minority group" if it becomes powerful enough.

The members of minority groups are entitled to their individual human rights, but they usually claim certain rights as members of a group as well. Depending on the particular group, these might include claims for cultural and political self-determination, land, compensation for dispossession, control of natural resources or access to religious sites.

🄰 Identifying some " minority groups"

Help the class develop a definition of "Minority group".

- Are they always in a minority mathematically?
- In what ways do minorities usually differ from the majority or dominant population?

Brainstorm with the class a list of contemporary "minority groups", starting with the local community. Be sure to include minorities based on class, ability, sexual orientation and other non-racial factors. Do these minority groups experience discrimination? In what ways?

Seniors students could eventually do case studies to find out about the size, location, history, culture, contemporary living conditions and key claims of specific minority groups.

- What are some circumstances that create minority groups in a population (e.g. indigenous peoples, immigrants, refugees, migrant workers)?

(UDHR articles 1, 2; CRC articles 2, 29, 30)

🄱 Cultural identity/cultural diversity

Everyone has a cultural identity, of which they are often unconscious because it is so much a part of them. However, in countries with ethnic, religious or linguistic minorities or

minorities of indigenous origin, cultural identity often becomes a human rights issue, especially when a more powerful group seeks to impose its culture on less powerful groups.

The Convention on the Rights of the Child pays particular attention to a child's right to his/her cultural identity. Article 29 guarantees a child an education that develops respect for his or her culture, language and values.

Article 30 especially recognizes the right of children of minority communities and indigenous populations to enjoy their own culture and practise their religion and language and article 31 recognizes a child's right to participate fully in cultural and artistic life.

UNESCO's *Universal Declaration on Cultural Diversity* emphasizes the link between cultural identity and diversity: "Culture takes diverse forms across time and space. This diversity is embodied in the uniqueness and plurality of the identities of the groups and societies making up humankind. As a source of exchange, innovation and creativity, cultural diversity is as necessary for humankind as biodiversity is for nature" (article 1).

Examine your own community.

- Are there cultural minorities?
- Is their culture respected?
- Do they participate freely and publicly in their culture, or are they expected to do so only privately or not at all?
- Does your school encourage respect for the culture of minority groups?

Discuss:

- Why is the right to cultural identity so important? Why is it important to preserve, develop and appreciate different cultures?
- Why do dominant groups often seek to impose their culture on minority groups?

(UDHR article 26; CRC articles 29, 30, 31)

ⓒ Minority group speakers

Invite members of a particular "minority group" to speak in class, perhaps under the auspices of its Human Rights Club. Prepare students by helping them to recognize their stereotyped expectations and to prepare useful questions. How can students best participate in promoting justice, freedom and equality in these particular cases?

(UDHR article 26; CRC articles 29, 30)

4. Discrimination – gender

Article 2 of the Universal Declaration proclaims the validity of human rights "without distinction of any kind". It goes on to make specific mention of a number of labels that are used to draw arbitrary lines between peoples. One of these is sex, and there is good reason to be specific, since sex discrimination ("sexism") remains one of the most pervasive sources of social injustice.

Sexism, like racism, may involve every aspect of culture and society. It is reflected in people's attitudes, many of them unconscious, which further that discrimination. To deny one sex full enjoyment of human rights is in effect to imply that that sex is not fully human.

Ⓐ Sex or gender?

Explain the difference between sex (biologically determined factors) and gender (culturally determined factors). Divide students into two teams and ask each to make a list of differences between males and females, some based on sex (e.g. adult men have beards; women live longer) and others based on gender (e.g. men are better at mathematics; women are timid). Each team in turn reads one of its characteristics and the panel must decide whether it is a difference based on sex or gender. Of course, disagreements will arise (e.g. are men naturally more aggressive?) but the resulting discussion will help students to recognize their own gender stereotypes. Examine the classroom, textbooks, media and community for examples of gender stereotyping.

(UDHR article 2; CRC article 2)

Ⓑ Who's who?

Have students survey the books and other materials they encounter at school:

• Are there the same number of references to males and females?

- Are female characters shown as brave decision-takers, physically capable, adventurous, creative and interested in a wide range of careers?
- Are male characters shown as humane, caring people, who can be helpful, who express their emotions, who are free of the fear that others might not think them "manly"?
- Do the men and women respect each other as equals?
- Do the men take an active part in parenting and house-keeping tasks?
- Do the women take an active role outside the home and, if so, in other than traditionally female occupations (e.g. teachers, nurses, secretaries) or unpaid or poorly paid jobs?

(UDHR article 2; CRC articles 2, 29)

Ⓒ Gender bender

Take a familiar story (e.g. from a novel, film, TV series or folk tale) and retell it with the gender of the characters switched. Discuss the effects of this gender switch.

(UDHR article 2; CRC article 2, 29)

Ⓓ What I like/What I do[11]

Ask students to write out answers to these questions about themselves:

1. Three things that my sex is supposed to do that I like.
2. Three things that my sex is supposed to do that I don't like.
3. Three things that I would like to do or be if I were of the other sex.

Ask students to share their lists with a partner of the same sex. Then ask each pair to share with a pair of the opposite sex (or in same-sex classrooms, with another pair).

---

[11] Adapted from *Local Action/Global Change: Learning about the Human Rights of Women and Girls* by Julie Mertus, Nancy Flowers and Mallika Dutt (UNIFEM, 1999).

Discuss the results. How does this community respond to people who don't conform to gender expectations? Do gender expectations limit people's human rights?

(UDHR article 2; CRC article 2)

▣ Making decisions

Ask students to brainstorm some important decisions a family has to make that affect all its members. Next to each decision, write whether it is made mainly by men, women or a combination. Discuss the differences in the kinds of decisions that males and females make in the family.

Next ask students to list some important decisions affecting the whole population that were made in their community in the last few years (e.g. starting a new club or team, building or closing a hospital, allotting land, increasing bus fares). Assign each small group one of these decisions to analyse:

• What are the gender implications of these decisions? Do they have any particular impact on women and girls? On men and boys?

• Next to each decision, write the name of the body that made the decision and the approximate percentage of males and females in that body.

• How might the decision be different if the decision-making body were composed of an equal number of males and females?

(UDHR articles 2, 21; CRC articles 2, 12)

▣ The non-sexist classroom

Most of the suggestions made for the non-racist classroom (See "2. Discrimination – colour or race" above) can be adopted to promote a non-sexist one. Seek help from wherever possible in breaking down gender stereotypes. Never allow exclusion based on sex. Always ask: what is fair? Acquaint students with the Convention on the Elimination of All Forms of Discrimination against Women (CEDAW).

Research has shown that teachers themselves can be potential sources of discrimination against girls, giving more attention to boys and calling on boys to speak twice as often as girls. In many classrooms boys are praised for their curiosity and assertiveness while girls are praised for their neatness, promptness and ability to follow instructions. Most teachers in these studies were unaware of their preference for boys and dismayed by the evidence.

The media, especially advertisements, provide good material for gender analysis. A close scrutiny of the school curriculum and textbooks is also advised (and see the activity *Who's who?* above).

- Does "history" give serious attention to the role of women as well as men?
- Does "economics" discuss women in the labour market (home or outside the home)?
- Does "law" look at women and property?
- Does "government" look at female under-representation?
- Does "science" give due weight to what women have done?
- Are girls encouraged to excel at mathematics, science and computers?
- How sexist is the teaching of "literature", "language and "the arts"?

Examine too the extra-curricular life of the school:

- Are girls given equal opportunities for leadership in clubs and elected offices? For representing the school publicly?
- Are there school-sponsored activities from which girls are excluded?
- Do girls have the same access to sports facilities and athletic teams as boys?
- Do girls feel safe from sexual harassment or physical threats at school?
- Are prizes, scholarships, financial assistance and other awards equally available to girls?

(UDHR articles 2, 26; CRC articles 2, 29)

5. Discrimination – disability

Practical work in the community outside school with people who are physically or intellectually disadvantaged is the best activity if students want to understand the issues involved.

A Speakers on disability

Invite people with particular disabilities to speak to the class, perhaps under the auspices of its Human Rights Club. They can explain the difficulties they encounter, the lessons they have learned as a result and what their specific rights might be. Stress the fact that people with disabilities are human first and disadvantaged second.

(UDHR articles 1, 2; CRC articles 2, 23)

B One school for all

Have the class examine the school and its environment and work out how accessible it is to people with particular disabilities.

Discuss:

- What changes would they recommend?
- What could your school do to promote the Declaration on the Rights of Disabled Persons and the Declaration on the Rights of Mentally Retarded Persons, proclaimed by the United Nations in 1975 and 1971 respectively?

(UDHR articles 1, 2; CRC articles 2, 23)

The right to education

Although everyone has the right to education, many never receive an education that fulfills article 29 of the Convention on the Rights of the Child and fosters "the development of the child's personality, talents and mental and physical abilities to their fullest potential" **(CRC, article 29.1).** Millions of children never have the opportunity to attend school at all. Many factors exclude them, such as their social status, their sex, or poverty which forces them to work to survive. Lack of education also limits their ability to enjoy other human rights.

Who is not in our school?

Ask students to consider what young people are not represented in their school, for example:

- many girls or boys?
- children with physical disabilities?
- children with mental disabilities?
- children who have been in trouble with the law or the school authorities?
- children who are orphaned?
- homeless children?
- children who are parents and/or are married?
- children of migrant workers?
- refugee children?
- children of minority groups in the community?
- poor children whose families need them to work?

For each group mentioned as absent from their school, ask:

- Why don't these children attend this school? Should they? Why or why not?
- Do they attend school elsewhere?
- What about children who cannot physically attend a school? How do they get an education?

If some children named attend different schools, ask:

- Why do these children attend a different school from yours?
- Where is this school? Can children get there easily?
- Must families pay for their children to attend this school? What if the parents cannot afford this alternative school?
- Do you think children get a good education there?

Ask how the right to education can be made available to those children who do not attend school (e.g. poor children whose families need them to work; girls who marry or have children while still of school age). Whose responsibility is it to ensure that they receive an education?

If possible, have students research and perhaps visit some schools for students with special needs. Have students discuss or write about whether these alternative schools meet the standards of the Convention of the Rights of the Child regarding the child's right to education. What can they do to advocate for the rights of all children to an education?

(UDHR article 26; CRC articles 28, 29)

B What if you couldn' t read?

Ask students to make a list of all the times they read something in a normal day: at home, at school, in the community or anywhere. They should include such "unconscious reading" as that done while using a computer, watching television and walking in the neighbourhood.

Ask students to compare their lists and discuss:

- How would your life be affected if you couldn't read?
- What activities would you be unable to do or do well?
- How could illiteracy affect the health, safety and security of you and your family?
- How would you be affected if you couldn't read and you were a
  - Mother? / Father?
  - Factory worker?
  - Agricultural worker?
  - Shop owner?
  - Soldier?
  - Citizen?

C Education as a human right

The right to education illustrates the principle of the interdependency of human rights. Ask the class to consider each of the thirty articles of the UDHR and/or the summarized version of the Convention of the Rights of the Child and ask "How would your ability to enjoy this right be different if you had no education?" **(e.g. UDHR article 21, the right to participate in government and in free elections; or CRC article 13, freedom of expression)**

Point out that, in the year 2000, of more than 850 million illiterate adults in the world, nearly two thirds were women. In addition, among the approximately 113 million children in the world who are not benefiting from primary education, 60 per cent are girls.[12] Ask students to explain these statistics. How does this fact affect the human rights of women and girls?

The right to learn your rights

Explain that education about and for human rights is itself an internationally agreed human right (see Chapter One of this booklet). Ask students:

- What do people need to know about human rights?
- Why is human rights education important? Do some people need it more than others? If so, who? And why?
- How should human rights be taught?
- How do human rights differ from other school subjects? (e.g. they involve action as well as knowledge)?
- How can students themselves learn about human rights?

(UDHR article 26; CRC articles 17, 29)

Development and the environment

Where do you live? Everywhere, the issues of development, human rights and the environment are interdependent, since development is meant to be people-centred, participatory and environmentally sound. It involves not just economic growth, but equitable distribution, enhancement of people's capabilities and widening of their choices. It gives top priority to poverty elimination, integration of women

---

[12] UNESCO, "Education for All Year 2000 Assessment".

into the development process, self-reliance and self-determination of people and Governments, and protection of the rights of indigenous people.

The strong link between human rights and development has figured prominently in United Nations deliberations for more than half a century. In 1986, the right to development was made explicit in article 1 of the United Nations *Declaration on the Right to Development*, which states that "the right to development is an inalienable human right by virtue of which every human person and all peoples are entitled to participate in, contribute to, and enjoy economic, social, cultural and political development, in which all human rights and fundamental freedoms can be fully realized". The right to development includes:

- full sovereignty over natural resources

- self-determination

- popular participation in development

- equality of opportunity

- the creation of favourable conditions for the enjoyment of other civil, political, economic, social and cultural rights.

Students may have a different understanding and experience of these issues, depending on the part of the world in which they live.

Teachers working with students who live daily under conditions of material deprivation may want to base their activities on the realities at hand and relate them as closely as possible to those of the world system. They may want to consider the prospects for progressive development and the steps necessary to achieve it.

Teachers working with materially privileged students may want to foster their responsiveness to claims for development and self-determination and to provide practical examples of how to facilitate them. Students may research the role of international cooperation by non-governmental organizations and intergovernmental agencies such as the United Nations Development Programme and the United Nations Environment Programme in fostering the right to development and the environment.

A Food

Ask students to keep a record of everything they eat and drink in a day. Analyse what they learn in terms of what their bodies need to survive and grow (i.e. carbohydrates, fats, proteins, minerals, vitamins and water).

Choose one meal and trace its components back to the people who produced, processed, transported and prepared them. This study might be combined with field trips to the sources that supply local markets and grocery stores.

Choose something from the daily diet – preferably something unfamiliar – that grows readily nearby. Have the class, working in pairs, grow an example of it in a can, pot or school garden. Determine why some students have more success with their plants than others. Invite someone with a

good knowledge of gardens or crops to talk to the class about plant care. Start a class garden in which all students can work and share the produce. Hold brainstorming sessions to discuss possible improvements. For example, is the method of cultivation the most suitable? Are there other ways of controlling pests? How could the system of sharing the work be made more efficient and cooperative?

Parallels could be drawn between the class work and the situation in other parts of the world. A school in an urban area might try to arrange with a school in a rural area to exchange visits and share particular experiences (in this case, their respective relationships to food production and distribution).

(UDHR article 25; CRC articles 24, 27)

B Water

Fresh water is scarce in the world and becoming even scarcer. Students who live in an arid area will be fully aware of this condition. Have the students calculate how much water they use in a day by making a chart that indicates drinking, washing, etc. Have them research where the water they use comes from.

Water carries wastes and organisms that cause
Sanitary water management (both supply and dis
essential to communal well-being. Have the students
or in small groups – research the water supply and d.
system of their school and suggest how it might be impr.
This can be done for the whole community as well. Wh.
anyone, is responsible for the safety of the water they use?

(UDHR article 25; CRC articles 24, 27)

[c] An adequate standard of living

Adequate food and water are basic development priorities. Article 25 of the Universal Declaration includes specific reference to food as part of the right to a standard of living adequate for health and well-being. Article 27 of the Convention on the Rights of the Child further guarantees every child the right to a standard of living adequate for her or his physical, mental, spiritual, moral and social development. These rights in turn are a concern of such bodies as the United Nations Children's Fund (UNICEF) and the Food and Agriculture Organization of the United Nations (FAO) and have a bearing also on national security and world peace.

Ask students to research the minimum requirements for food and water necessary for survival and for well-being. What happens when a child lacks a standard of living adequate for full development?

Assign students countries with contrasting levels of development to research using United Nations statistics from publications such as UNICEF's *State of the World's Children* or the United Nations Development Programme's *Human Development Report*. Have each student present a profile of an average person from that country (e.g. life expectancy, income, diet, and access to clean water). Discuss the effects of such differences on the development of individuals as well as nations and regions.

Teachers of materially privileged students might ask them to find out about poverty in their own communities. Discuss who bears responsibility for protecting people from the effects of poverty.

(UDHR articles 23, 25; CRC articles 6, 27)

⒟ Housing

Houses directly reflect such things as local climate and geography, family structure and status, cultural and religious preferences and the availability of building materials. Brainstorm with the class a list of all the things that a house should have and then get them to design one that has these features. Have them describe and explain the features of what they have designed.

- How does the design reflect their values and culture?
- How might local house designs be modified and improved to conserve resources like water and power, and to minimize pollution?
- What could be the specific needs of family members with physical disabilities?

If there are homeless people in the community, discuss and research who is homeless and why.

- Who has responsibility for the homeless?
- Is homelessness a human rights issue?
- What can be done to address it?

(UDHR article 25; CRC article 27)

⒠ Population

In many parts of the world, the effects of population growth are very clear. In other areas they are less obvious. The impact of this phenomenon is universal, however. Statistics show how the world population is expanding at an exponential rate and how this growth will affect the environment and competition for resources. It is important for students to think about population growth and the issues behind it.

The topic of population also provides opportunities to discuss conflicting rights and the relationship of the individual to the State. Ask students to research and debate the policies of different States on family size, either encouraging or discouraging many children.

- Do these policies conflict with individual rights?
- If so, how should these conflicts be resolved?

(UDHR article 16)

ⓕ Work

As the world economy changes, so does the nature of the world's work. In developed countries, for example, industrialization brought urbanization, with fewer people now living in the country and producing agricultural products. In large cities a greater number of people work in service industries. Where there is not enough work to employ all those looking for jobs, people tend to move around the world to improve their economic opportunities. Migration patterns both within and between countries are often related to work, as are patterns of economic development. Countries should endeavour to integrate their agricultural, industrial, financial and trade policies so as to maximize the productive capacity of their people.

As part of becoming adult, many students will already be investigating different types of work. Bringing a wide range of working people into the classroom helps to broaden students' awareness. Even better, take students into different work environments so that they can actually see what is involved. If possible, ask the students what areas of work interest them and organize field trips.

Of particular interest are issues relating to child labour: should children's working age, hours of work and kind of work be regulated? The practical and moral issues involved provide important areas for reflection and research. Students might compare the 1999 Convention concerning the Prohibition of the Worst Forms of Child Labour (No. 182) of the International Labour Organization (a United Nations

chap. 3

agency specialized in human and labour rights) with the provisions of the Convention on the Rights of the Child.

Examination of child labour and labour practices can generally also lead students to explore the subject of consumer responsibility and the connection between human rights and global trade practices. (See "Business and human rights" below).

Student projects on work (e.g. patterns of local, national and international employment; how "work" is changing at one or all of these levels; how "workers" organize to protect their rights) can produce important learning outcomes. Conventions, recommendations and reports of the International Labour Organization provide useful information about work and human rights.

(UDHR articles 23, 24; CRC articles 31, 32, 36)

⊞ Energy

Doing anything takes energy. The more you do, the more you need. Brainstorm with the class all the possible sources of energy, such as sunlight, food, coal, gas and electricity. Ask students to record all the forms of energy they use in a day. Trace where each comes from and how it gets to those who use it. Is it a "renewable" source? Discuss the environmental effects of these forms of energy as well.

Make an energy inventory of the school. Are there ways in which energy is wasted? Make suggestions for saving energy. The same procedure could also be applied to the home, the community, the region and the whole world.

Set group projects to design – even build – devices which can provide energy for the community. What is available locally that can be used for this purpose: wind? sun? water? fossil fuels? wastes?

(UDHR article 25; CRC article 27)

⊞ Health

Health is a fundamental human right, and a basic goal of global development. Numerous resolutions of the World Health Organization (WHO), a United Nations agency specialized in

this area, have reaffirmed this goal and the need to reduce the gross inequalities in the health status of the world's people. The planning and the implementation of primary health care requires both individual and collective action to ensure that while health is provided for all, most resources go to those most in need. Exploring local, national and global health care systems suggest diverse and interesting projects. Most countries include health education in their school curricula, providing students with basic information about nutrition, physiology and the causes and prevention of disease. A local doctor or visiting health worker can be a good resource as a guest speaker or for relevant facts and ideas. Arrange field trips to hospitals and community health projects.

The general topic of health also raises other important human rights issues: discrimination against girls in health care, the health implications of child labour and child marriage, the right to information about reproductive health, the negative effects of environmental pollution and malnutrition, and the positive effects of education on health.

**(UDHR articles 2, 19, 25;
CRC articles 2, 3, 17, 24, 17, 28)**

Economic development and interrelatedness

The Universal Declaration and the Convention on the Rights of the Child contain a number of articles that affirm the rights of human beings to a decent standard of living. Whether these are realized or not is a complex issue which depends also on national resources, industrial development, economic priorities and political will. The achievement of economic development – which has both national and international implications – clearly has a bearing on the implementation of those rights.

The world's resources and its disposable wealth are unevenly distributed. Why is this so? Any adequate answer would have to describe and explain the geography and the history of world society and of its political economy as a whole.

A Local/global

Ask students to search through newspapers and news magazines for articles that describe how another part of the world is having an impact on the local community or how their country is having an impact on another part of the world (e.g. environmental, economic, health or political problems; exchanges of food, fashion, music or other forms of culture; migration; imports or exports, especially of food or resources). Ask the class to make some categories for the kind of links they have found (e.g. trade, culture, tourism, environment) and label each article with the relevant category.

Post a map of the world and ask students to group their articles around it by category. Draw a line with arrows or stretch a piece of yarn between the country of origin and the country impacting or being impacted by it.

Discuss:

* Which parts of the world had the most links? The least? Why?
* What kinds of links were most frequent?
* What does this activity show about our global interdependence?

(UDHR articles 13, 19; CRC article 17)

B Working life

Describe a working environment (e.g. a factory, a plantation or a farm) where the workers have decided to make a number of requests to the owners or managers. They want more say in how the place is run. They also want better wages, better provision for sickness and injury, more attention to workplace safety, the chance to set up an education programme and longer rest periods.

Form the class into two groups: workers and officials. Have them negotiate, each side sending delegates who report back. Refer students to the conventions of the International

Labour Organization for the relevant information on workers' rights. Then repeat the activity but reverse the roles.

(UDHR article 23; CRC article 32)

Effects webs

Young people today need to understand the world as a complex web of interdependent relationships and appreciate the delicate balance among the parts of that web, so that changing any one part affects the whole. For example, environmental pollution in one place can affect food chains, health, living conditions and livelihoods in many other places. Issues too are interrelated. Poverty may be caused by many factors, and any efforts to eradicate poverty must consider all of them.

To help students appreciate the complexity of these interrelationships, divide the class into an even number of small groups and assign each a statement, with at least two groups receiving the same statement. These sentences should express either a fact (e.g. "In ___ at least 30 per cent of the population is infected with the HIV-AIDS virus") or a "what if" statement (e.g. "What if women owned as much property as men?"). Each group writes its statement at the top of a piece of chart paper. Below the statement, they should write three consequences of that statement (e.g. "The parents of many children will die", "Many children will be born infected with HIV-AIDS", "National health care services will be overburdened by so many sick people"). Then below each of these three statements, write three consequences resulting from each (e.g. "The parents of many children will die" might lead to "Families and social services will be overburdened caring for orphaned children", "There will be fewer workers available", "There will be many children without parents to raise them properly"). The result is a graphic web of effects that could be developed even further. Ask groups with the same statement to compare and discuss their work. Display the charts and make a "gallery walk" so students can explain their webs to other members of the class.

Discuss the human rights implications of these webs and how single issues affect many aspects of society and many different countries.

(UDHR article 28; CRC article 3)

🄳 Speakers on development issues

Invite someone involved in development issues to speak to the class, perhaps under the auspices of its Human Rights Club. Prepare for the visit by giving students background information and helping them formulate questions for the speaker. Follow up by assigning class groups to study aspects of what was discussed (e.g. geographic areas, specific sections of the community, special issues that affect everyone, such as modernization, bureaucratization, globalization, urbanization and changes in cultural values).

(UDHR articles 19, 25; CRC articles 6, 27)

Business and human rights

At its inception in the mid-twentieth century, the Universal Declaration of Human Rights and the developing human rights framework mainly addressed how Governments behaved toward their citizens. However, with the emergence of the global economy, many businesses today surpass Governments in their finances, power and influence over the lives of people. While Governments are legally accountable to their citizens, businesses, especially those that operate in many different countries around the world, have little legal public accountability, except to their stockholders. As a result, these transnational corporations are increasingly at the centre of human rights issues.

🄰 Should businesses be accountable?

Discuss these issues:

- In what ways could a large transnational business violate the human rights of its employees? Of people in general?
- In what ways could such a business use its influence to promote human rights?
- Why might it benefit a business to adhere to human rights standards? Why might that be a disadvantage?

- Should a business be accountable for observing human rights standards?

- How can citizens and non-governmental organizations (NGOs) put pressure on businesses to adhere to human rights standards?

(UDHR article 28; CRC articles 3, 6)

⬛B A corporate code of conduct

Some businesses have responded to the growing pressure to conform to human rights standards by creating corporate codes of conduct to be used by all their companies and business partners.

Imagine you have been hired by a large transnational corporation (e.g. a garment manufacturer, an oil company) to help them draft a code of conduct. Working in small groups, draft a list of principles that the business should follow in all aspects of its work. Include human rights, labour practices and environmental considerations. Compare all the drafts and combine them to create a final document.

You might want to compare your list with the "Global Compact", a list of principles launched by United Nations Secretary-General Kofi Annan in 1999 (available at http://www.unglobalcompact.org or by contacting the United Nations).

(UDHR articles 3, 28; CRC articles 3, 6)

⬛C Speakers from the business community

Invite representatives from local business associations (e.g. chamber of commerce, Rotary Club, bankers or merchants association) as well as public authorities and non-governmental organizations involved in fair/ethical trade initiatives, perhaps under the auspices of the class's Human Rights Club, to discuss how local commerce is affected by the global economy and to explain their view on corporate accountability for human rights.

(UDHR articles 19, 23, 25; CRC articles 3, 6, 17, 27)

Understanding the United Nations

Article 26 of the Universal Declaration of Human Rights states that education "shall ... promote the activities of the United Nations for the maintenance of peace". A model United Nations, a simulation of the United Nations system in which students assume the roles of "ambassadors" of the United Nations Member States, is a powerful educational tool to help students understand the limitations and potential of the United Nations.

Most model United Nations programmes are based on three distinct steps:

1. Preparation: Students research three basic subjects:
   (a) The United Nations and its work;
   (b) The Government, policies and interests of a United Nations Member State;
   (c) The global issues on the agenda.
   The research and study should lead to the development of a "position paper" or resolution and a negotiation strategy for the assigned Member State.

2. Participation: The research comes to life as students become "ambassadors" of Member States and practise the skills of public speaking, listening, time management, negotiation and consultation.

3. Evaluation: Careful debriefing and assessment is essential to bring the exercise to a close. Some criteria should be developed for success in each aspect of the simulation (e.g. research, presentation, negotiation).

The role of the teacher is that not of an expert but a guide who can assist students with research and analysis. The following is a simplified version of a model United Nations activity. See the resource list in annex 5 for further information about model United Nations programmes. Contact the World Federation of United Nations Associations for further information about model United Nations programmes (see annex 4).

A model United Nations simulation

Select a few current issues of global importance for students to focus on. Assign individuals or groups of students to represent and research a variety of United Nations Member States. Explain that the goals of their research are to understand the assigned country and how it would regard the key issues.

When students have had time to complete their research, ask each "ambassador" to write a resolution for the "General Assembly" on one of the key issues of importance in their country or region. The resolution should include a detailed description of the problem and a plan to improve the situation, including what role the United Nations should play. Students will need to convince others that their resolution benefits everyone and deserves to be considered. Encourage students to compare their resolutions and begin to seek supporters and/or co-sponsors. Explain that they need to be prepared to amend their resolutions and build consensus to get them passed.

Hold a mock United Nations forum. Seat students in a circle with the names of their countries in front of them. The teacher or a capable student serves as "Secretary-General". Establish some rules of order for the forum (e.g. each person is addressed as "The Ambassador from ___" ; no one may speak unless recognized by the "Secretary-General").

The "Secretary-General" calls for resolutions to be presented, debated, questioned and voted upon. After discussion on a potential resolution, anyone may move that the resolution be put to the vote. For a motion to pass, it must be seconded by any other "ambassador". A two-thirds majority is needed to pass a resolution.

Conclude the simulation with a written or oral evaluation, including both a self-evaluation and an assessment of what students learned about the United Nations and its role in world affairs.

(UDHR articles 1, 28, 30; CRC article 3)

Creating a human rights community

One of the ultimate goals of human rights education is the creation of a genuine human rights culture. To do so, students must learn to evaluate real-life experience in human rights terms, starting with their own behaviour and the immediate community in which they live. They need to make an honest assessment of how the reality they experience every day conforms to human rights principles and then to take active responsibility for improving their community.

Taking the human rights temperature of your school[13]

Ask students to evaluate their school's human rights climate, i.e. take its "temperature", by completing the survey below. Record and discuss their findings:

- In which areas does your school seem to be promoting human rights principles?
- In which areas do there seem to be human rights problems?
- How do you explain the existence of such problematic conditions? Are they related to discrimination? To participation in decision-making? Who benefits and who loses/suffers from these human rights violations?
- Have you or any other members of the community contributed to the existing climate, either to improve or to worsen it?
- What needs to be done to improve the human rights climate in your school?

Develop an action plan as a class, identifying goals, strategies and responsibilities.

[13] Adapted from *Social and Economic Justice: A Human Rights Perspective* by David Shiman (University of Minnesota Human Rights Resource Center, 1999).

Taking the human rights temperature of your school

Directions: Read each statement and evaluate how accurately it describes your school community. Keep in mind all members of your school: students, teachers, administrators, staff. Add up your score to determine the overall assessment for your school.

Rating scale:

1	2	3	4	?
Never	Rarely	Often	Always	DN
(No/False)			(Yes/True)	Don't know

1. Members of the school community are not discriminated against because of their race, sex, family background, disability, religion or life style.
   (UDHR articles 2, 16; CRC articles 2, 23) ❑

2. My school is a place where I am safe and secure.
   (UDHR articles 3, 5; CRC articles 6, 37) ❑

3. All students receive equal information and encouragement about academic and career opportunities.
   (UDHR articles 2, 26; CRC articles 2, 29) ❑

4. My school provides equal access, resources, activities and accommodation for everyone.
   (UDHR articles 2, 7; CRC article 2) ❑

5. Members of my school community will oppose discriminatory actions, materials or words in the school.
   (UDHR articles 2, 3, 7, 28, 29; CRC articles 2, 3, 6, 30) ❑

6. When someone violates the rights of another person, the violator is helped to learn how to change her/his behaviour.
   (UDHR article 26; CRC articles 28, 29) ❑

7. Members of my school community care about my full human as well as academic development and try to help me when I am in need.
   (UDHR articles 3, 22, 26, 29; CRC articles 3, 6, 27, 28, 29, 31) ❑

8. When conflicts arise, we try to resolve them in non-violent and collaborative ways.

   (UDHR articles 3, 28; CRC articles 3, 13, 19, 29, 37) ❑

9. The school has policies and procedures regarding discrimination and uses them when incidents occur.

   (UDHR articles 3, 7; CRC articles 3, 29) ❑

10. In matters related to discipline, everyone is assured of fair, impartial treatment in the determination of guilt and assignment of punishment.

   (UDHR articles 6, 7, 8, 9, 10; CRC articles 28, 40) ❑

11. No one in our school is subjected to degrading treatment or punishment.

   (UDHR article 5; CRC articles 13, 16,19, 28) ❑

12. Someone accused of wrong-doing is presumed innocent until proved guilty.

   (UDHR article 11; CRC articles 16, 28, 40) ❑

13. My personal space and possessions are respected.

   (UDHR articles 12, 17; CRC article 16) ❑

14. My school community welcomes students, teachers, administrators and staff from diverse backgrounds and cultures, including people not born in this country.

   (UDHR articles 2, 6, 13, 14, 15; CRC articles 2, 29, 30, 31) ❑

15. I have the liberty to express my beliefs and ideas without fear of discrimination.

   (UDHR article 19; CRC articles 13, 14) ❑

16. Members of my school can produce and disseminate publications without fear of censorship or punishment.

   (UDHR article 19; CRC article 13) ❑

17. Diverse perspectives (e.g. gender, race/ethnicity, ideological) are represented in courses, textbooks, assemblies, libraries and classroom instruction.

   (UDHR articles 2, 19, 27; CRC articles 17, 29, 30) ❑

18. I have the opportunity to participate in cultural activities at the school and my cultural identity, language and values are respected.

(UDHR articles 19, 27, 28; CRC articles 29, 30, 31) ❑

19. Members of my school have the opportunity to participate in democratic decision-making to develop school policies and rules.

(UDHR articles 20, 21, 23; CRC articles 13, 15) ❑

20. Members of my school have the right to form associations within the school to advocate for their rights or the rights of others.

(UDHR articles 19, 20, 23; CRC article 15) ❑

21. Members of my school encourage each other to learn about societal and global problems related to justice, ecology, poverty and peace.

(UDHR preamble, articles 26, 29; CRC article 29) ❑

22. Members of my school encourage each other to organize and take action to address problems related to justice, ecology, poverty and peace.

(UDHR preamble, articles 20, 29; CRC article 29) ❑

23. Members of my school community are able to take adequate rest/recess time during the school day and work reasonable hours under fair work conditions.

(UDHR articles 23, 24; CRC articles 31, 32) ❑

24. Employees in my school are paid enough to have a standard of living adequate for the health and well-being of themselves and their families.

(UDHR articles 22, 25; CRC article 27) ❑

25. I take responsibility in my school to ensure that people do not discriminate against others.

(UDHR articles 1, 29; CRC article 29) ❑

Total ❑

Possible temperature = 100 human rights degrees

Your school's temperature = _____ human rights degrees

Just a beginning...

ABC: Teaching Human Rights is a beginning, not an end. It contains proposals, not prescriptions. Its purpose is to stimulate discussion and ideas and thus to help children to develop an objective, basic understanding of rights and obligations, so as to apply human rights principles to the fullest extent of our human existence.

This booklet is intended to empower and inspire teachers, motivating them to find the most effective teaching methods and strategies for integrating human rights into the curriculum and culture of their schools. Teachers are encouraged to seek out other human rights educators and to form networks for sharing ideas and experiences.

However, all human rights education efforts share some basic features:

- A core value system of universal human rights principles, such as human dignity and equality;

- A content rooted in central human rights documents, such as the Universal Declaration of Human Rights and the Convention on the Rights of the Child;

- An acceptance of the universality, indivisibility and interdependence of human rights;

- An awareness of the interrelationship between human rights and individual and State responsibilities;

- An understanding of human rights as an evolving process, responsive to the developing understanding of human needs, and the role of citizens and non-governmental organizations in bringing their concerns to the international arena. For example, in 1948 when the Universal Declaration of Human Rights was adopted, few people were concerned about environmental pollution. Now clean air and water are increasingly viewed as a basic human right and international legal instruments to address environmental concerns are under discussion.

Last but not least, students need to recognize that human rights are not about violations occurring to other people somewhere else. Human rights concern the right of all people, in all their diversity, to achieve "the full development of the human personality" in a "social and international order in which the rights and freedoms set forth in [the Universal] Declaration can be fully realized" **(UDHR, articles 26 and 28)**.

Encourage students to consider how they might best use what they have learned to promote and protect human rights in their own communities. Such action would build upon many of the activities in this booklet that provide for practical application of human rights principles in the society at large. It would consolidate those lessons and guide students in building the skills they need to make a contribution outside the class and school, both now and in adult life.

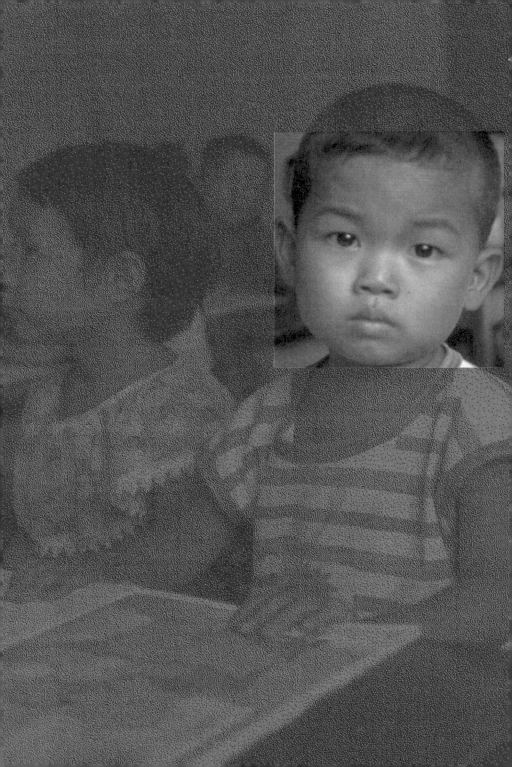

Universal Declaration of Human Rights (1948)[a]

The plain language version is given only as a guide. For an exact rendering of each principle, refer students to the original. This "simplified" version is based on a French text prepared in 1978 for the World Association for the School as an Instrument of Peace by a Research Group of the University of Geneva under the responsibility of Prof. L. Massarenti. In preparing the French "simplified" version, the Group used a basic vocabulary of 2,500 words in use in the French-speaking part of Switzerland. The English translation of the French version was prepared by the United Nations. Teachers may adopt this methodology when they translate the text of the Universal Declaration into the language in use in their region.

---

[a] See <http://www.ohchr.org> for the text of the Universal Declaration of Human Rights in more than 300 different languages.

Original text	Plain language version

...

Article 1

All human beings are born free and equal in dignity and rights. They are endowed with reason and conscience and should act towards one another in a spirit of brotherhood.

When children are born, they are free and each should be treated in the same way. They have reason and conscience and should act towards one another in a friendly manner.

Article 2

Everyone is entitled to all the rights and freedoms set forth in this Declaration, without distinction of any kind, such as race, colour, sex, language, religion, political or other opinion, national or social origin, property, birth or other status. Furthermore, no distinction shall be made on the basis of the political, jurisdictional or international status of the country or territory to which a person belongs, whether it be independent, trust, non-self-governing or under any other limitation of sovereignty.

Everyone can claim the following rights, despite
- a different sex
- a different skin colour
- speaking a different language
- thinking different things
- believing in another religion
- owning more or less
- being born in another social group
- coming from another country.
It also makes no difference whether the country you live in is independent or not.

Article 3

Everyone has the right to life, liberty and security of person.

You have the right to live, and to live in freedom and safety.

Article 4

No one shall be held in slavery or servitude; slavery and the slave trade shall be prohibited in all their forms.

Nobody has the right to treat you as his or her slave and you should not make anyone your slave.

Article 5

No one shall be subjected to torture or to cruel, inhuman or degrading treatment or punishment.

Nobody has the right to torture you.

Article 6

Everyone has the right to recognition everywhere as a person before the law.

You should be legally protected in the same way everywhere, and like everyone else.

Article 7

All are equal before the law and are entitled without any discrimination to equal protection of the law. All are entitled to equal protection

The law is the same for everyone; it should be applied in the same way to all.

against any discrimination in violation of this Declaration and against any incitement to such discrimination.

Article 8

Everyone has the right to an effective remedy by the competent national tribunals for acts violating the fundamental rights granted him by the constitution or by law.

You should be able to ask for legal help when the rights your country grants you are not respected.

Article 9

No one shall be subjected to arbitrary arrest, detention or exile.

Nobody has the right to put you in prison, to keep you there, or to send you away from your country unjustly, or without a good reason.

Article 10

Everyone is entitled in full equality to a fair and public hearing by an independent and impartial tribunal, in the determination of his rights and obligations and of any criminal charge against him.

If you must go on trial this should be done in public. The people who try you should not let themselves be influenced by others.

Article 11

1. Everyone charged with a penal offence has the right to be presumed innocent until proved guilty according to law in a public trial at which he has had all the guarantees necessary for his defence.
2. No one shall be held guilty of any penal offence on account of any act or omission which did not constitute a penal offence, under national or international law, at the time when it was committed. Nor shall a heavier penalty be imposed than the one that was applicable at the time the penal offence was committed.

You should be considered innocent until it can be proved that you are guilty. If you are accused of a crime, you should always have the right to defend yourself. Nobody has the right to condemn you and punish you for something you have not done.

Article 12

No one shall be subjected to arbitrary interference with his privacy, family, home or correspondence, nor to attacks upon his honour and reputation. Everyone has the right to the protection of the law against such interference or attacks.

You have the right to ask to be protected if someone tries to harm your good name, enter your house, open your letters, or bother you or your family without a good reason.

Article 13

1. Everyone has the right to freedom of movement and residence within the borders of each State.

You have the right to come and go as you wish within your country. You

2. Everyone has the right to leave any country, including his own, and to return to his country.

have the right to leave your country to go to another one; and you should be able to return to your country if you want.

Article 14

1. Everyone has the right to seek and to enjoy in other countries asylum from persecution.
2. This right may not be invoked in the case of prosecutions genuinely arising from non-political crimes or from acts contrary to the purposes and principles of the United Nations.

If someone hurts you, you have the right to go to another country and ask it to protect you.
You lose this right if you have killed someone and if you yourself do not respect what is written here.

Article 15

1. Everyone has the right to a nationality.
2. No one shall be arbitrarily deprived of his nationality nor denied the right to change his nationality.

You have the right to belong to a country and nobody can prevent you, without a good reason, from belonging to another country if you wish.

Article 16

1. Men and women of full age, without any limitation due to race, nationality or religion, have the right to marry and to found a family. They are entitled to equal rights as to marriage, during marriage and at its dissolution.
2. Marriage shall be entered into only with the free and full consent of the intending spouses.
3. The family is the natural and fundamental group unit of society and is entitled to protection by society and the State.

As soon as a person is legally entitled, he or she has the right to marry and have a family. Neither the colour of your skin, nor the country you come from nor your religion should be impediments to doing this. Men and women have the same rights when they are married and also when they are separated.
Nobody should force a person to marry. The Government of your country should protect your family and its members.

Article 17

1. Everyone has the right to own property alone as well as in association with others.
2. No one shall be arbitrarily deprived of his property.

You have the right to own things and nobody has the right to take these from you without a good reason.

Article 18

Everyone has the right to freedom of thought, conscience and religion; this right includes freedom to change his religion or belief, and freedom, either alone or in community with others

You have the right to profess your religion freely, to change it, and to practise it either on your own or with other people.

and in public or private, to manifest his religion or belief in teaching, practice, worship and observance.

Article 19

Everyone has the right to freedom of opinion and expression; this right includes freedom to hold opinions without interference and to seek receive and impart information and ideas though any media and regardless of frontiers.

You have the right to think what you want, and to say what you like, and nobody should forbid you from doing so.
You should be able to share your ideas – also with people from any other country.

Article 20

1. Everyone has the right to freedom of peaceful assembly and association.
2. No one may be compelled to belong to an association.

You have the right to organize peaceful meetings or to take part in meetings in a peaceful way. It is wrong to force someone to belong to a group.

Article 21

1. Everyone has the right to take part in the government of his country, directly or through freely chosen representatives.
2. Everyone has the right of equal access to public service in his country.
3. The will of the people shall be the basis of the authority of government; this will shall be expressed in periodic and genuine elections which shall be by universal and equal suffrage and shall be held by secrete vote or by equivalent free voting procedures.

You have the right to take part in your country's political affairs either by belonging to the Government yourself of by choosing politicians who have the same ideas as you.
Governments should be voted for regularly and voting should be secret. You should get a vote and all votes should be equal. You also have the same right to join the public service as anyone else.

Article 22

Everyone, as a member of society, has the right to social security and is entitled to realization, through national effort and international co-operation and in accordance with the organization and resources of each State, of the economic, social and cultural rights indispensable for his dignity and the free development of his personality.

The society in which you live should help you to develop and to make the most of all the advantages (culture, work, social welfare) that are offered to you and to all the men and women in your country.

Article 23

1. Everyone has the right to work, to free choice of employment, to just and favourable condi-

You have the right to work, to be free to choose your work, and to get

Original text	Plain language version
tions of work and to protection against unemployment. 2. Everyone, without any discrimination, has the right to equal pay for equal work. 3. Every one who works has the right to just and favourable remuneration ensuring for himself and his family an existence worthy of human dignity, and supplemented, if necessary, by other means of social protection. 4. Everyone has the right to form and to join trade unions for the protection of his interests.	*a salary that allows you to live and support your family. If a man and a woman do the same work, they should get the same pay. All people who work have the right to join together to defend their interests.*

Article 24

Everyone has the right to rest and leisure, including reasonable limitation of working hours and periodic holidays with pay.	*Each work day should not be too long, since everyone has the right to rest and should be able to take regular paid holidays.*

Article 25

1. Everyone has the right to a standard of living adequate for the health and well-being of himself and of his family, including foods, clothing, housing and medical care and necessary social services, and the right to security in the event of unemployment, sickness, disability, widowhood, old age or other lack of livelihood in circumstances beyond his control. 2. Motherhood and childhood are entitled to special care and assistance. All children, whether born in or out of wedlock, shall enjoy the same social protection.	*You have the right to have whatever you need so that you and your family: do not fall ill; do not go hungry; have clothes and a house; and are helped if you are out of work, if you are ill, if you are old, if your wife or husband is dead, or if you do not earn a living for any other reason you cannot help.* *Both a mother who is going to have a baby and her baby should get special help. All children have the same rights, whether or not the mother is married.*

Article 26

1. Everyone has the right to education. Education shall be free, at least in the elementary and fundamental stages. Elementary education shall be compulsory. Technical and professional education shall be made generally available and higher education shall be equally accessible to all on the basis of merit. 2. Education shall be directed to the full development of the human personality and to the strengthening of respect for human rights and fundamental freedoms. It shall promote understanding, tolerance and friendship among all	*You have the right to go to school and everyone should go to school. Primary schooling should be free. You should be able to learn a profession or continue your studies as far as you wish. At school, you should be able to develop all your talents and you should be taught to get on with others, whatever their race, their religion or the country they come from. Your parents have the right to choose how and what you will be taught at school.*

nations, racial or religious groups, and shall further the activities of the United Nations for the maintenance of peace.

3. Parents have a prior right to choose the kind of education that shall be given to their children.

Article 27

1. Everyone has the right freely to participate in the cultural life of the community, to enjoy the arts and to share in scientific advancement and its benefits.

2. Everyone has the right to the protection of the moral and material interests resulting from any scientific, literary or artistic production of which he is the author.

You have the right to share in your community's arts and sciences, and in any good they do. Your works as an artist, a writer or a scientist should be protected, and you should be able to benefit from them.

Article 28

Everyone is entitled to a social and international order in which the rights and freedoms set forth in this Declaration can be fully realized.

To make sure that your rights will be respected, there must be an "order" that can protect them. This "order" should be local and worldwide.

Article 29

1. Everyone has duties to the community in which alone the free and full development of his personality is possible.

2. In the exercise of his rights and freedoms, everyone shall be subject only to such limitations as are determined by law solely for the purpose of securing due recognition and respect for the rights and freedoms of others and of meeting the just requirements of morality, public order and the general welfare in a democratic society.

3. These rights and freedoms may in no case be exercised contrary to the purposes and principles of the United Nations.

You have duties towards the community within which your personality can fully develop. The law should guarantee human rights. It should allow everyone to respect others and to be respected.

Article 30

Nothing in this Declaration may be interpreted as implying for any State, group or person any right to engage in any activity or to perform any act aimed at the destruction of any of the rights and freedoms set forth herein.

No society and no human being in any part of the world should act in such a way as to destroy the rights that you have just been reading about.

Universal Declaration of Human Rights (1948)

Annex 2

Convention on the Rights of the Child

Adopted by the General Assembly
of the United Nations
on 20 November 1989

Original text

PREAMBLE

. . . .

The States Parties to the present Convention,

Considering that, in accordance with the principles proclaimed in the Charter of the United Nations, recognition of the inherent dignity and of the equal and inalienable rights of all members of the human family is the foundation of freedom, justice and peace in the world,

Bearing in mind that the peoples of the United Nations have, in the Charter, reaffirmed their faith in fundamental human rights and in the dignity and worth of the human person, and have determined to promote social progress and better standards of life in larger freedom,

Recognizing that the United Nations has, in the Universal Declaration of Human Rights and in the International Covenants on Human Rights, proclaimed and agreed that everyone is entitled to all the rights and freedoms set forth therein, without distinction of any kind, such as race, colour, sex, language, religion, political or other opinion, national or social origin, property, birth or other status,

Recalling that, in the Universal Declaration of Human Rights, the United Nations has proclaimed that childhood is entitled to special care and assistance,

Convinced that the family, as the fundamental group of society and the natural environment for the growth and well-being of all its members and particularly children, should be afforded the necessary protection and assistance so that it can fully assume its responsibilities within the community,

Recognizing that the child, for the full and harmonious development of his or her personality, should grow up in a family environment, in an atmosphere of happiness, love and understanding,

Considering that the child should be fully prepared to live an individual life in society, and brought up in the spirit of the ideals proclaimed in the Charter of the United Nations, and in particular in the spirit of peace, dignity, tolerance, freedom, equality and solidarity,

Unofficial summary [a]

. . . .

The preamble recalls the basic principles of the United Nations and specific provisions of certain relevant human rights treaties and proclamations. It reaffirms the fact that children, because of their vulnerability, need special care and protection, and it places special emphasis on the primary caring and protective responsibility of the family. It also reaffirms the need for legal and other protection of the child before and after birth, the importance of respect for the cultural values of the child's community, and the vital role of international cooperation in securing children's rights.

[a] Source: UNICEF.

Bearing in mind that the need to extend particular care to the child has been stated in the Geneva Declaration of the Rights of the Child of 1924 and in the Declaration of the Rights of the Child adopted by the United Nations on 20 November 1959 and recognized in the Universal Declaration of Human Rights, in the International Covenant on Civil and Political Rights (in particular in articles 23 and 24), in the International Covenant on Economic, Social and Cultural Rights (in particular in article 10) and in the statutes and relevant instruments of specialized agencies and international organizations concerned with the welfare of children,

Bearing in mind that, as indicated in the Declaration of the Rights of the Child, "the child, by reason of his physical and mental immaturity, needs special safeguards and care, including appropriate legal protection, before as well as after birth",

Recalling the provisions of the Declaration on Social and Legal Principles relating to the Protection and Welfare of Children, with Special Reference to Foster Placement and Adoption Nationally and Internationally; the United Nations Standard Minimum Rules for the Administration of Juvenile Justice ("The Beijing Rules"); and the Declaration on the Protection of Women and Children in Emergency and Armed Conflict,

Recognizing that, in all countries in the world, there are children living in exceptionally difficult conditions, and that such children need special consideration,

Taking due account of the importance of the traditions and cultural values of each people for the protection and harmonious development of the child,

Recognizing the importance of international cooperation for improving the living conditions of children in every country, in particular in the developing countries,

Have agreed as follows:

Original text

Unofficial summary

PART I

Article 1

For the purposes of the present Convention, a child means every human being below the age of 18 years unless, under the law applicable to the child, majority is attained earlier.

Definition of a child

A child is recognized as a person under 18, unless national laws recognize the age of majority earlier.

Article 2

1. States Parties shall respect and ensure the rights set forth in the present Convention to each child within their jurisdiction without discrimination of any kind, irrespective of the child's or his or her parent's or legal guardian's race, colour, sex, language, religion, political or other opinion, national, ethnic or social origin, property, disability, birth or other status.

2. States Parties shall take all appropriate measures to ensure that the child is protected against all forms of discrimination or punishment on the basis of the status, activities, expressed opinions, or beliefs of the child's parents, legal guardians, or family members.

Non-discrimination

All rights apply to all children without exception. It is the State's obligation to protect children from any form of discrimination and to take positive action to promote their rights.

Article 3

1. In all actions concerning children, whether undertaken by public or private social welfare institutions, courts of law, administrative authorities or legislative bodies, the best interests of the child shall be a primary consideration.

2. States Parties undertake to ensure the child such protection and care as is necessary for his or her wellbeing, taking into account the rights and duties of his or her parents, legal guardians, or other individuals legally responsible for him or her, and, to this end, shall take all appropriate legislative and administrative measures.

3. States Parties shall ensure that the institutions, services and facilities responsible for the care or protection of children shall conform with the standards established by competent authorities, particularly in the areas of safety, health, in the number and suitability of their staff, as well as competent supervision.

Best interests of the child

All actions concerning the child shall take full account of his or her best interests. The State shall provide the child with adequate care when parents, or others charged with that responsibility, fail to do so.

Original text	Unofficial summary

Article 4

States Parties shall undertake all appropriate legislative, administrative, and other measures for the implementation of the rights recognized in the present Convention. With regard to economic, social and cultural rights, States Parties shall undertake such measures to the maximum extent of their available resources and, where needed, within the framework of international co-operation.

Implementation of rights

The State must do all it can to implement the rights contained in the Convention.

Article 5

States Parties shall respect the responsibilities, rights and duties of parents or, where applicable, the members of the extended family or community as provided for by local custom, legal guardians or other persons legally responsible for the child, to provide, in a manner consistent with the evolving capacities of the child, appropriate direction and guidance in the exercise by the child of the rights recognized in the present Convention.

Parental guidance and the child's evolving capacities

The State must respect the rights and responsibilities of parents and the extended family to provide guidance for the child which is appropriate to her or his evolving capacities.

Article 6

1. States Parties recognize that every child has the inherent right to life.

2. States Parties shall ensure to the maximum extent possible the survival and development of the child.

Survival and development

Every child has the inherent right to life, and the State has an obligation to ensure the child's survival and development.

Article 7

1. The child shall be registered immediately after birth and shall have the right from birth to a name, the right to acquire a nationality and, as far as possible, the right to know and be cared for by his or her parents.

2. States Parties shall ensure the implementation of these rights in accordance with their national law and their obligations under the relevant international instruments in this field, in particular where the child would otherwise be stateless.

Name and nationality

The child has the right to a name at birth. The child also has the right to acquire a nationality and, as far as possible, to know his or her parents and be cared for by them.

Article 8

1. States Parties undertake to respect the right of the child to preserve his or her identity, including nationality, name and family relations as recog-

Preservation of identity

The State has an obligation to protect, and if necessary, reestablish basic aspects of the child's identity.

Original text

nized by law without unlawful interference.

2. Where a child is illegally deprived of some or all of the elements of his or her identity, States Parties shall provide appropriate assistance and protection, with a view to speedily re-establishing his or her identity.

Article 9

1. States Parties shall ensure that a child shall not be separated from his or her parents against their will, except when competent authorities subject to judicial review determine, in accordance with applicable law and procedures, that such separation is necessary for the best interests of the child. Such determination may be necessary in a particular case such as one involving abuse or neglect of the child by the parents, or one where the parents are living separately and a decision must be made as to the child's place of residence.

2. In any proceedings pursuant to paragraph 1 of the present article, all interested parties shall be given an opportunity to participate in the proceedings and make their views known.

3. States Parties shall respect the right of the child who is separated from one or both parents to maintain personal relations and direct contact with both parents on a regular basis, except if it is contrary to the child's best interests.

4. Where such separation results from any action initiated by a State Party, such as the detention, imprisonment, exile, deportation or death (including death arising from any cause while the person is in the custody of the State) of one or both parents or of the child, that State Party shall, upon request, provide the parents, the child or, if appropriate, another member of the family with the essential information concerning the whereabouts of the absent member(s) of the family unless the provision of the information would be detrimental to the well-being of the child. States Parties shall further ensure that the submission of such a request shall of itself entail no adverse consequences for the person(s) concerned.

Unofficial summary

This includes name, nationality and family ties.

Separation from parents

The child has a right to live with his or her parents unless this is deemed to be incompatible with the child's best interests. The child also has the right to maintain contact with both parents if separated from one or both.

Article 10

Family reunification

1. In accordance with the obligation of States Parties under article 9, paragraph 1, applications by a child or his or her parents to enter or leave a State Party for the purpose of family reunification shall be dealt with by States Parties in a positive, humane and expeditious manner. States Parties shall further ensure that the submission of such a request shall entail no adverse consequences for the applicants and for the members of their family.

Children and their parents have the right to leave any country and to enter their own for purposes of reunion or the maintenance of the child-parent relationship.

2. A child whose parents reside in different States shall have the right to maintain on a regular basis, save in exceptional circumstances personal relations and direct contacts with both parents. Towards that end and in accordance with the obligation of States Parties under article 9, paragraph 1, States Parties shall respect the right of the child and his or her parents to leave any country, including their own, and to enter their own country. The right to leave any country shall be subject only to such restrictions as are prescribed by law and which are necessary to protect the national security, public order (*ordre public*), public health or morals or the rights and freedoms of others and are consistent with the other rights recognized in the present Convention.

Article 11

Illicit transfer and non-return

1. States Parties shall take measures to combat the illicit transfer and non-return of children abroad.

The State has an obligation to prevent and remedy the kidnapping or retention of children abroad by a parent or third party.

2. To this end, States Parties shall promote the conclusion of bilateral or multilateral agreements or accession to existing agreements.

Article 12

The child's opinion

1. States Parties shall assure to the child who is capable of forming his or her own views the right to express those views freely in all matters affecting the child, the views of the child being given due weight in accordance with the age and maturity of the child.

The child has the right to express his or her opinion freely and to have that opinion taken into account in any matter or procedure affecting the child.

2. For this purpose, the child shall in particular be provided the opportunity to be heard in any judi-

Convention on the Rights of the Child (1989)

cial and administrative proceedings affecting the child, either directly, or through a representative or an appropriate body, in a manner consistent with the procedural rules of national law.

Article 13

1. The child shall have the right to freedom of expression; this right shall include freedom to seek, receive and impart information and ideas of all kinds, regardless of frontiers, either orally, in writing or in print, in the form of art, or through any other media of the child's choice.

2. The exercise of this right may be subject to certain restrictions, but these shall only be such as are provided by law and are necessary:

(a) For respect of the rights or reputations of others; or

(b) For the protection of national security or of public order (*ordre public*), or of public health or morals.

Article 14

1. States Parties shall respect the right of the child to freedom of thought, conscience and religion.

2. States Parties shall respect the rights and duties of the parents and, when applicable, legal guardians, to provide direction to the child in the exercise of his or her right in a manner consistent with the evolving capacities of the child.

3. Freedom to manifest one's religion or beliefs may be subject only to such limitations as are prescribed by law and are necessary to protect public safety, order, health or morals, or the fundamental rights and freedoms of others.

Article 15

1. States Parties recognize the rights of the child to freedom of association and to freedom of peaceful assembly.

2. No restrictions may be placed on the exercise of these rights other than those imposed in conformity with the law and which are necessary in a democratic society in the interests of national security or public safety, public order (*ordre public*), the pro-

Freedom of expression

The child has the right to express his or her views, obtain information, make ideas or information known, regardless of frontiers.

Freedom of thought, conscience and religion

The State shall respect the child's right to freedom of thought, conscience and religion, subject to appropriate parental guidance.

Freedom of association

Children have a right to meet with others, and to join or form associations.

tection of public health or morals or the protection of the rights and freedoms of others.

Article 16

1. No child shall be subjected to arbitrary or unlawful interference with his or her privacy, family, home or correspondence, nor to unlawful attacks on his or her honour and reputation.

2. The child has the right to the protection of the law against such interference or attacks.

Article 17

States Parties recognize the important function performed by the mass media and shall ensure that the child has access to information and material from a diversity of national and international sources, especially those aimed at the promotion of his or her social, spiritual and moral well-being and physical and mental health. To this end, States Parties shall:

(a) Encourage the mass media to disseminate information and material of social and cultural benefit to the child and in accordance with the spirit of article 29;

(b) Encourage international co-operation in the production, exchange and dissemination of such information and material from a diversity of cultural, national and international sources;

(c) Encourage the production and dissemination of children's books;

(d) Encourage the mass media to have particular regard to the linguistic needs of the child who belongs to a minority group or who is indigenous;

(e) Encourage the development of appropriate guidelines for the protection of the child from information and material injurious to his or her well-being, bearing in mind the provisions of articles 13 and 18.

Article 18

1. States Parties shall use their best efforts to ensure recognition of the principle that both parents have common responsibilities for the

Protection of privacy

Children have the right to protection from interference with privacy, family, home and correspondence, and from libel or slander.

Access to appropriate information

The State shall ensure the accessibility to children of information and material from a diversity of sources, and it shall encourage the mass media to disseminate information which is of social and cultural benefit to the child, and take steps to protect him or her from harmful materials.

Parental responsibilities

Parents have joint primary responsibility for raising the child, and the State shall support them in this. The

upbringing and development of the child. Parents or, as the case may be, legal guardians, have the primary responsibility for the upbringing and development of the child. The best interests of the child will be their basic concern.

2. For the purpose of guaranteeing and promoting the rights set forth in the present Convention, States Parties shall render appropriate assistance to parents and legal guardians in the performance of their childrearing responsibilities and shall ensure the development of institutions, facilities and services for the care of children.

3. States Parties shall take all appropriate measures to ensure that children of working parents have the right to benefit from child-care services and facilities for which they are eligible.

State shall provide appropriate assistance to parents in child-raising.

Article 19

1. States Parties shall take all appropriate legislative, administrative, social and educational measures to protect the child from all forms of physical or mental violence, injury or abuse, neglect or negligent treatment, maltreatment or exploitation, including sexual abuse, while in the care of parent(s), legal guardian(s) or any other person who has the care of the child.

2. Such protective measures should, as appropriate, include effective procedures for the establishment of social programmes to provide necessary support for the child and for those who have the care of the child, as well as for other forms of prevention and for identification, reporting, referral, investigation, treatment and follow-up of instances of child maltreatment described heretofore, and, as appropriate, for judicial involvement.

Protection from abuse and neglect

The State shall protect the child from all forms of maltreatment by parents or others responsible for the care of the child and establish appropriate social programmes for the prevention of abuse and the treatment of victims.

Article 20

1. A child temporarily or permanently deprived of his or her family environment, or in whose own best interests cannot be allowed to remain in that environment, shall be entitled to special protection and assistance provided by the State.

2. States Parties shall in accordance with their national laws ensure alternative care for such a child.

Protection of a child without family

The State is obliged to provide special protection for a child deprived of the family environment and to ensure that appropriate alternative family care or institutional placement is available in such cases. Efforts to meet this obligation shall pay due regard to the child's cultural background.

3. Such care could include, *inter alia*, foster placement, *kafala* of Islamic law, adoption, or if necessary placement in suitable institutions for the care of children. When considering solutions, due regard shall be paid to the desirability of continuity in a child's upbringing and to the child's ethnic, religious, cultural and linguistic background.

Article 21

States Parties that recognize and/or permit the system of adoption shall ensure that the best interests of the child shall be the paramount consideration and they shall:

(a) Ensure that the adoption of a child is authorized only by competent authorities who determine, in accordance with applicable law and procedures and on the basis of all pertinent and reliable information, that the adoption is permissible in view of the child's status concerning parents, relatives and legal guardians and that, if required, the persons concerned have given their informed consent to the adoption on the basis of such counselling as may be necessary;

(b) Recognize that inter-country adoption may be considered as an alternative means of child's care, if the child cannot be placed in a foster or an adoptive family or cannot in any suitable manner be cared for in the child's country of origin;

(c) Ensure that the child concerned by intercountry adoption enjoys safeguards and standards equivalent to those existing in the case of national adoption;

(d) Take all appropriate measures to ensure that, in intercountry adoption, the placement does not result in improper financial gain for those involved in it;

(e) Promote, where appropriate, the objectives of the present article by concluding bilateral or multilateral arrangements or agreements, and endeavour, within this framework, to ensure that the placement of the child in another country is carried out by competent authorities or organs.

Adoption

In countries where adoption is recognized and/or allowed, it shall only be carried out in the best interests of the child, and then only with the authorization of competent authorities, and safeguards for the child.

Convention on the Rights of the Child (1989)

Original text

Article 22

....

1. States Parties shall take appropriate measures to ensure that a child who is seeking refugee status or who is considered a refugee in accordance with applicable international or domestic law and procedures shall, whether unaccompanied or accompanied by his or her parents or by any other person, receive appropriate protection and humanitarian assistance in the enjoyment of applicable rights set forth in the present Convention and in other international human rights or humanitarian instruments to which the said States are Parties.

2. For this purpose, States Parties shall provide, as they consider appropriate, co-operation in any efforts by the United Nations and other competent intergovernmental organizations or non-governmental organizations co-operating with the United Nations to protect and assist such a child and to trace the parents or other members of the family of any refugee child in order to obtain information necessary for reunification with his or her family. In cases where no parents or other members of the family can be found, the child shall be accorded the same protection as any other child permanently or temporarily deprived of his or her family environment for any reason, as set forth in the present Convention.

Article 23

....

1. States Parties recognize that a mentally or physically disabled child should enjoy a full and decent life, in conditions which ensure dignity, promote self-reliance, and facilitate the child's active participation in the community.

2. States Parties recognize the right of the disabled child to special care and shall encourage and ensure the extension, subject to available resources, to the eligible child and those responsible for his or her care, of assistance for which application is made and which is appropriate to the child's condition and to the circumstances of the parents or others caring for the child.

3. Recognizing the special needs of a disabled child, assistance extended in accordance with

Unofficial summary

Refugee children

....

Special protection shall be granted to a refugee child or to a child seeking refugee status. It is the State's obligation to cooperate with competent organizations which provide such protection and assistance.

Disabled children

....

A disabled child has the right to special care, education and training to help him or her enjoy a full and decent life in dignity and achieve the greatest degree of self-reliance and social integration possible.

paragraph 2 of the present article shall be provided free of charge, whenever possible, taking into account the financial resources of the parents or others caring for the child, and shall be designed to ensure that the disabled child has effective access to and receives education, training, health care services, rehabilitation services, preparation for employment and recreation opportunities in a manner conducive to the child's achieving the fullest possible social integration and individual development, including his or her cultural and spiritual development.

4. States Parties shall promote, in the spirit of international co-operation, the exchange of appropriate information in the field of preventive health care and of medical, psychological and functional treatment of disabled children, including dissemination of and access to information concerning methods of rehabilitation, education and vocational services, with the aim of enabling States Parties to improve their capabilities and skills and to widen their experience in these areas. In this regard, particular account shall be taken of the needs of developing countries.

Article 24

1. States Parties recognize the right of the child to the enjoyment of the highest attainable standard of health and to facilities for the treatment of illness and rehabilitation of health. States Parties shall strive to ensure that no child is deprived of his or her right of access to such health care services.

2. States Parties shall pursue full implementation of this right and, in particular, shall take appropriate measures:

(a) To diminish infant and child mortality;

(b) To ensure the provision of necessary medical assistance and health care to all children with emphasis on the development of primary health care;

(c) To combat disease and malnutrition including within the framework of primary health care, through *inter alia* the application of readily available technology and through the provision

Health and health services

The child has a right to the highest standard of health and medical care attainable. States shall place special emphasis on the provision of primary and preventive health care, public health education and the reduction of infant mortality. They shall encourage international co-operation in this regard and strive to see that no child is deprived of access to effective health services.

of adequate nutritious foods and clean drinking water, taking into consideration the dangers and risks of environmental pollution;

(d) To ensure appropriate pre-natal and post-natal health care for mothers;

(e) To ensure that all segments of society, in particular parents and children, are informed, have access to education and are supported in the use of basic knowledge of child health and nutrition, the advantages of breast-feeding, hygiene and environmental sanitation and the prevention of accidents;

(f) To develop preventive health care, guidance for parents and family planning education and services.

3. States Parties shall take all effective and appropriate measures with a view to abolishing traditional practices prejudicial to the health of children.

4. States Parties undertake to promote and encourage international co-operation with a view to achieving progressively the full realization of the right recognized in the present article. In this regard, particular account shall be taken of the needs of developing countries.

Article 25

States Parties recognize the right of a child who has been placed by the competent authorities for the purposes of care, protection or treatment of his or her physical or mental health, to a periodic review of the treatment provided to the child and all other circumstances relevant to his or her placement.

Article 26

1. States Parties shall recognize for every child the right to benefit from social security, including social insurance, and shall take the necessary measures to achieve the full realization of this right in accordance with their national law.

2. The benefits should, where appropriate, be granted, taking into account the resources and the circumstances of the child and persons hav-

Periodic review of placement

A child who is placed by the State for reasons of care, protection or treatment is entitled to have that placement evaluated regularly.

Social security

The child has the right to benefit from social security including social insurance.

ing responsibility for the maintenance of the child, as well as any other consideration relevant to an application for benefits made by or on behalf of the child.

Article 27

Standard of living

1. States Parties recognize the right of every child to a standard of living adequate for the child's physical, mental, spiritual, moral and social development.

2. The parent(s) or others responsible for the child have the primary responsibility to secure, within their abilities and financial capacities, the conditions of living necessary for the child's development.

3. States Parties, in accordance with national conditions and within their means, shall take appropriate measures to assist parents and others responsible for the child to implement this right and shall in case of need provide material assistance and support programmes, particularly with regard to nutrition, clothing and housing.

4. States Parties shall take all appropriate measures to secure the recovery of maintenance for the child from the parents or other persons having financial responsibility for the child, both within the State Party and from abroad. In particular, where the person having financial responsibility for the child lives in a State different from that of the child, States Parties shall promote the accession to international agreements or the conclusion of such agreements, as well as the making of other appropriate arrangements.

Every child has the right to a standard of living adequate for his or her physical, mental, spiritual, moral and social development. Parents have the primary responsibility to ensure that the child has an adequate standard of living. The State's duty is to ensure that this responsibility can be fulfilled, and is. State responsibility can include material assistance to parents and their children.

Article 28

Education

1. States Parties recognize the right of the child to education, and with a view to achieving this right progressively and on the basis of equal opportunity, they shall, in particular:

(a) Make primary education compulsory and available free to all;

(b) Encourage the development of different forms of secondary education, including general and vocational education, make them available

The child has a right to education, and the State's duty is to ensure that primary education is free and compulsory, to encourage different forms of secondary education accessible to every child and to make higher education available to all on the basis of capacity. School discipline shall be consistent with the child's rights and dignity. The State shall engage in

Original text

and accessible to every child, and take appropriate measures such as the introduction of free education and offering financial assistance in case of need;

(c) Make higher education accessible to all on the basis of capacity by every appropriate means;

(d) Make educational and vocational information and guidance available and accessible to all children;

(e) Take measures to encourage regular attendance at schools and the reduction of drop-out rates.

2. States Parties shall take all appropriate measures to ensure that school discipline is administered in a manner consistent with the child's human dignity and in conformity with the present Convention.

3. States Parties shall promote and encourage international co-operation in matters relating to education, in particular with a view to contributing to the elimination of ignorance and illiteracy throughout the world and facilitating access to scientific and technical knowledge and modern teaching methods. In this regard, particular account shall be taken of the needs of developing countries.

Article 29

1. States Parties agree that the education of the child shall be directed to:

(a) The development of the child's personality, talents and mental and physical abilities to their fullest potential;

(b) The development of respect for human rights and fundamental freedoms, and for the principles enshrined in the Charter of the United Nations;

(c) The development of respect for the child's parents, his or her own cultural identity, language and values, for the national values of the country in which the child is living, the country from which he or she may originate, and for civilizations different from his or her own;

Unofficial summary

international cooperation to implement this right.

Aims of education

Education shall aim at developing the child's personality, talents and mental and physical abilities to the fullest extent. Education shall prepare the child for an active adult life in a free society and foster respect for the child's parents, his or her own cultural identity, language and values, and for the cultural background and values of others.

(d) The preparation of the child for responsible life in a free society, in the spirit of understanding, peace, tolerance, equality of sexes, and friendship among all peoples, ethnic, national and religious groups and persons of indigenous origin;

(e) The development of respect for the natural environment.

2. No part of the present article or article 28 shall be construed so as to interfere with the liberty of individuals and bodies to establish and direct educational institutions, subject always to the observance of the principles set forth in paragraph 1 of the present article and to the requirements that the education given in such institutions shall conform to such minimum standards as may be laid down by the State.

Article 30

In those States in which ethnic, religious or linguistic minorities or persons of indigenous origin exist, a child belonging to such a minority or who is indigenous shall not be denied the right, in community with other members of his or her group, to enjoy his or her own culture, to profess and practise his or her own religion, or to use his or her own language.

Article 31

1. States Parties recognize the right of the child to rest and leisure, to engage in play and recreational activities appropriate to the age of the child and to participate freely in cultural life and the arts.

2. States Parties shall respect and promote the right of the child to participate fully in cultural and artistic life and shall encourage the provision of appropriate and equal opportunities for cultural, artistic, recreational and leisure activity.

Article 32

1. States Parties recognize the right of the child to be protected from economic exploitation and from performing any work that is likely to be hazardous or to interfere with the child's education,

Children of minorities or indigenous populations

Children of minority communities and indigenous populations have the right to enjoy their own culture and to practise their own religion and language.

Leisure, recreation and cultural activities

The child has the right to leisure, play and participation in cultural and artistic activities.

Child labour

The child has the right to be protected from work that threatens his or her health, education or development. The State shall set minimum

Original text

or to be harmful to the child's health or physical, mental, spiritual, moral or social development.

2. States Parties shall take legislative, administrative, social and educational measures to ensure the implementation of the present article. To this end, and having regard to the relevant provisions of other international instruments, States Parties shall in particular:

(a) Provide for a minimum age or minimum ages for admissions to employment;

(b) Provide for appropriate regulation of the hours and conditions of employment;

(c) Provide for appropriate penalties or other sanctions to ensure the effective enforcement of the present article.

Article 33

States Parties shall take all appropriate measures, including legislative, administrative, social and educational measures, to protect children from the illicit use of narcotic drugs and psychotropic substances as defined in the relevant international treaties, and to prevent the use of children in the illicit production and trafficking of such substances.

Article 34

States Parties undertake to protect the child from all forms of sexual exploitation and sexual abuse. For these purposes, States Parties shall in particular take all appropriate national, bilateral and multilateral measures to prevent:

(a) The inducement or coercion of a child to engage in any unlawful sexual activity;

(b) The exploitative use of children in prostitution or other unlawful sexual practices;

(c) The exploitative use of children in pornographic performances and materials.

Article 35

States Parties shall take all appropriate national, bilateral and multilateral measures to prevent the abduction of, the sale of or traffic in children for any purpose or in any form.

Unofficial summary

ages for employment and regulate working conditions.

Drug abuse

Children have the right to protection from the use of narcotic and psychotropic drugs, and from being involved in their production or distribution.

Sexual exploitation

The State shall protect children from sexual exploitation and abuse, including prostitution and involvement in pornography.

Sale, trafficking and abduction

It is the State's obligation to make every effort to prevent the sale, trafficking and abduction of children.

Article 36

States Parties shall protect the child against all other forms of exploitation prejudicial to any aspects of the child's welfare.

Article 37

States Parties shall ensure that:
(a) No child shall be subjected to torture or other cruel, inhuman or degrading treatment or punishment. Neither capital punishment nor life imprisonment without possibility of release shall be imposed for offences committed by persons below 18 years of age;

(b) No child shall be deprived of his or her liberty unlawfully or arbitrarily. The arrest, detention or imprisonment of a child shall be in conformity with the law and shall be used only as a measure of last resort and for the shortest appropriate period of time;

(c) Every child deprived of liberty shall be treated with humanity and respect for the inherent dignity of the human person, and in a manner which takes into account the needs of persons of his or her age. In particular every child deprived of liberty shall be separated from adults unless it is considered in the child's best interest not to do so and shall have the right to maintain contact with his or her family through correspondence and visits, save in exceptional circumstances;

(d) Every child deprived of his or her liberty shall have the right to prompt access to legal and other appropriate assistance, as well as the right to challenge the legality of the deprivation of his or her liberty before a court or other competent, independent and impartial authority, and to a prompt decision on any such action.

Article 38

1. States Parties undertake to respect and to ensure respect for rules of international humanitarian law applicable to them in armed conflicts which are relevant to the child.

Other forms of exploitation

The child has the right to protection from all forms of exploitation prejudicial to any aspects of the child's welfare not covered in articles 32, 33, 34 and 35.

Torture and deprivation of liberty

No child shall be subjected to torture, cruel treatment or punishment, unlawful arrest or deprivation of liberty. Both capital punishment and life imprisonment without the possibility of release are prohibited for offences committed by persons below 18 years. Any child deprived of liberty shall be separated from adults unless it is considered in the child's best interests not to do so. A child who is detained shall have legal and other assistance as well as contact with the family.

Armed conflicts

States Parties shall take all feasible measures to ensure that children under 15 years of age have no direct part in hostilities. No child below

Original text

2. States Parties shall take all feasible measures to ensure that persons who have not attained the age of 15 years do not take a direct part in hostilities.

3. States Parties shall refrain from recruiting any person who has not attained the age of 15 years into their armed forces. In recruiting among those persons who have attained the age of 15 years but who have not attained the age of 18 years, States Parties shall endeavour to give priority to those who are oldest.

4. In accordance with their obligations under international humanitarian law to protect the civilian population in armed conflicts, States Parties shall take all feasible measures to ensure protection and care of children who are affected by an armed conflict.

Article 39

States Parties shall take all appropriate measures to promote physical and psychological recovery and social reintegration of a child victim of: any form of neglect, exploitation, or abuse; torture or any other form of cruel, inhuman or degrading treatment or punishment; or armed conflicts. Such recovery and reintegration shall take place in an environment which fosters the health, self-respect and dignity of the child.

Article 40

1. States Parties recognize the right of every child alleged as, accused of, or recognized as having infringed the penal law to be treated in a manner consistent with the promotion of the child's sense of dignity and worth, which reinforces the child's respect for the human rights and fundamental freedoms of others and which takes into account the child's age and the desirability of promoting the child's reintegration and the child's assuming a constructive role in society.

2. To this end, and having regard to the relevant provisions of international instruments, States Parties shall, in particular, ensure that:

(a) No child shall be alleged as, be accused of, or recognized as having infringed the penal law by

Unofficial summary

15 shall be recruited into the armed forces. States shall also ensure the protection and care of children who are affected by armed conflict as described in relevant international law.

Rehabilitative care

The State has an obligation to ensure that child victims of armed conflicts, torture, neglect, maltreatment or exploitation receive appropriate treatment for their recovery and social reintegration.

Administration of juvenile justice

A child in conflict with the law has the right to treatment which promotes the child's sense of dignity and worth, takes the child's age into account and aims at his or her reintegration into society. The child is entitled to basic guarantees as well as legal or other assistance for his or her defence. Judicial proceedings and institutional placements shall be avoided wherever possible.

reason of acts or omissions that were not prohibited by national or international law at the time
they were committed;

(b) Every child alleged as or accused of having
infringed the penal law has at least the following
guarantees:

(i) To be presumed innocent until proven guilty
according to law;

(ii) To be informed promptly and directly of the
charges against him or her, and, if appropriate,
through his or her parents or legal guardians,
and to have legal or other appropriate assistance
in the preparation and presentation of his or her
defence;

(iii) To have the matter determined without
delay by a competent, independent and impartial authority or judicial body in a fair hearing
according to law, in the presence of legal or
other appropriate assistance and, unless it is considered not to be in the best interest of the child,
in particular, taking into account his or her age
or situation, his or her parents or legal guardians;

(iv) Not to be compelled to give testimony or to
confess guilt; to examine or have examined
adverse witnesses and to obtain the participation
and examination of witnesses on his or her
behalf under conditions of equality;

(v) If considered to have infringed the penal law,
to have this decision and any measures imposed
in consequence thereof reviewed by a higher
competent, independent and impartial authority
or judicial body according to law;

(vi) To have the free assistance of an interpreter
if the child cannot understand or speak the language used;

(vii) To have his or her privacy fully respected at
all stages of the proceedings.

3. States Parties shall seek to promote the establishment of laws, procedures, authorities and
institutions specifically applicable to children
alleged as, accused of, or recognized as having
infringed the penal law, and, in particular:

(a) the establishment of a minimum age below

Convention on the Rights of the Child (1989)

which children shall be presumed not to have the capacity to infringe the penal law;

(b) whenever appropriate and desirable, measures for dealing with such children without resorting to judicial proceedings, providing that human rights and legal safeguards are fully respected.

4. A variety of dispositions, such as care, guidance and supervision orders; counselling; probation; foster care; education and vocational training programmes and other alternatives to institutional care shall be available to ensure that children are dealt with in a manner appropriate to their well-being and proportionate both to their circumstances and the offence.

Article 41
••

Nothing in the present Convention shall affect any provisions which are more conducive to the realization of the rights of the child and which may be contained in:

(a) The law of a State Party; or

(b) International law in force for that State.

PART II
Article 42
••

States Parties undertake to make the principles and provisions of the Convention widely known, by appropriate and active means, to adults and children alike.

Article 43
••

1. For the purpose of examining the progress made by States Parties in achieving the realization of the obligations undertaken in the present Convention, there shall be established a Committee on the Rights of the Child, which shall carry out the functions hereinafter provided.

2. The Committee shall consist of ten experts of high moral standing and recognized competence in the field covered by this Convention. The members of the Committee shall be elected by States Parties from among their nationals and shall serve in their personal capacity, consideration being

Respect for higher standards
••

Wherever standards set in applicable national and international law relevant to the rights of the child are higher than those in this Convention, the higher standard shall always apply.

Implementation and entry into force
••

The provisions of articles 42-54 notably foresee:
(i) the State's obligation to make the rights contained in this Convention widely known to both adults and children.
(ii) the setting up of a Committee on the Rights of the Child composed of ten experts, which will consider reports that States Parties to the Convention are to submit two years after ratification and every five years thereafter. The Convention enters into force – and the Committee would therefore be set up – once 20 countries have ratified it.
(iii) States Parties are to make their reports widely available to the general public.

given to equitable geographical distribution, as well as to the principal legal systems.

3. The members of the Committee shall be elected by secret ballot from a list of persons nominated by States Parties. Each State Party may nominate one person from among its own nationals.

4. The initial election to the Committee shall be held no later than six months after the date of the entry into force of the present Convention and thereafter every second year. At least four months before the date of each election, the Secretary-General of the United Nations shall address a letter to States Parties inviting them to submit their nominations within two months. The Secretary-General shall subsequently prepare a list in alphabetical order of all persons thus nominated, indicating States Parties which have nominated them, and shall submit it to the States Parties to the present Convention.

5. The elections shall be held at meetings of States Parties convened by the Secretary-General at United Nations Headquarters. At those meetings, for which two thirds of States Parties shall constitute a quorum, the persons elected to the Committee shall be those who obtain the largest number of votes and an absolute majority of the votes of the representatives of States Parties present and voting.

6. The members of the Committee shall be elected for a term of four years. They shall be eligible for reelection if renominated. The term of five of the members elected at the first election shall expire at the end of two years; immediately after the first election, the names of these five members shall be chosen by lot by the Chairman of the meeting.

7. If a member of the Committee dies or resigns or declares that for any other cause he or she can no longer perform the duties of the Committee, the State Party which nominated the member shall appoint another expert from among its nationals to serve for the remainder of the term, subject to the approval of the Committee.

8. The Committee shall establish its own rules of procedure.

(iv) The Committee may propose that special studies be undertaken on specific issues relating to the rights of the child, and may make its evaluations known to each State Party concerned as well as to the UN General Assembly.

(v) In order to "foster the effective implementation of the Convention and to encourage international cooperation", the specialized agencies of the UN – such as the International Labour Organization (ILO), World Health Organization (WHO) and United Nations Educational, Scientific and Cultural Organization (UNESCO) – and UNICEF would be able to attend the meetings of the Committee. Together with any other body recognized as 'competent', including non-governmental organizations (NGOs) in consultative status with the UN and UN organs such as the Office of the United Nations High Commissioner for Refugees (UNHCR), they can submit pertinent information to the Committee and be asked to advise on the optimal implementation of the Convention.

Convention on the Rights of the Child (1989)

9. The Committee shall elect its officers for a period of two years.

10. The meetings of the Committee shall normally be held at United Nations Headquarters or at any other convenient place as determined by the Committee. The Committee shall normally meet annually. The duration of the meetings of the Committee shall be determined, and reviewed, if necessary, by a meeting of the States Parties to the present Convention, subject to the approval of the General Assembly.

11. The Secretary-General of the United Nations shall provide the necessary staff and facilities for the effective performance of the functions of the Committee under the present Convention.

12. With the approval of the General Assembly, the members of the Committee established under the present Convention shall receive emoluments from the United Nations resources on such terms and conditions as the Assembly may decide.

Article 44

1. States Parties undertake to submit to the Committee, through the Secretary-General of the United Nations, reports on the measures they have adopted which give effect to the rights recognized herein and on the progress made on the enjoyment of those rights:

(a) Within two years of the entry into force of the Convention for the State Party concerned,

(b) Thereafter every five years.

2. Reports made under the present article shall indicate factors and difficulties, if any, affecting the degree of fulfilment of the obligations under the present Convention. Reports shall also contain sufficient information to provide the Committee with a comprehensive understanding of the implementation of the Convention in the country concerned.

3. A State Party which has submitted a comprehensive initial report to the Committee need not in its subsequent reports submitted in accordance with paragraph 1(b) of the present article repeat basic information previously provided.

4. The Committee may request from States Parties further information relevant to the implementation of the Convention.

5. The Committee shall submit to the General Assembly, through the Economic and Social Council, every two years, reports on its activities.

6. States Parties shall make their reports widely available to the public in their own countries.

Article 45

In order to foster the effective implementation of the Convention and to encourage international co-operation in the field covered by the Convention:

(a) The specialized agencies, the United Nations Children's Fund and other United Nations organs shall be entitled to be represented at the consideration of the implementation of such provisions of the present Convention as fall within the scope of their mandate. The Committee may invite the specialized agencies, the United Nations Children's Fund and other competent bodies as it may consider appropriate to provide expert advice on the implementation of the Convention in areas falling within the scope of their respective mandates. The Committee may invite the specialized agencies, the United Nations Children's Fund and other United Nations organs to submit reports on the implementation of the Convention in areas falling within the scope of their activities;

(b) The Committee shall transmit, as it may consider appropriate, to the specialized agencies, the United Nations Children's Fund and other competent bodies, any reports from States Parties that contain a request, or indicate a need, for technical advice or assistance, along with the Committee's observations and suggestions, if any, on these requests or indications;

(c) The Committee may recommend to the General Assembly to request the Secretary-General to undertake on its behalf studies on specific issues relating to the rights of the child;

(d) The Committee may make suggestions and general recommendations based on information received pursuant to articles 44 and 45 of the present Convention. Such suggestions and general recommendations shall be transmitted to any State Party concerned and reported to the General Assembly, together with comments, if any, from States Parties.

PART III

Article 46

The present Convention shall be open for signature by all States.

Article 47

The present Convention is subject to ratification. Instruments of ratification shall be deposited with the Secretary-General of the United Nations.

Article 48

The present Convention shall remain open for accession by any State. The instruments of accession shall be deposited with the Secretary-General of the United Nations.

Article 49

1. The present Convention shall enter into force on the thirtieth day following the date of deposit with the Secretary-General of the United Nations of the twentieth instrument of ratification or accession.

2. For each State ratifying or acceding to the Convention after the deposit of the twentieth instrument of ratification or accession, the Convention shall enter into force on the thirtieth day after the deposit by such State of its instrument of ratification or accession.

Article 50

1. Any State Party may propose an amendment and file it with the Secretary-General of the United Nations. The Secretary-General shall thereupon communicate the proposed amendment to States Parties, with a request that they

indicate whether they favour a conference of States Parties for the purpose of considering and voting upon the proposals. In the event that, within four months from the date of such communication, at least one third of the States Parties favour such a conference, the Secretary-General shall convene the conference under the auspices of the United Nations. Any amendment adopted by a majority of States Parties present and voting at the conference shall be submitted to the General Assembly for approval.

2. An amendment adopted in accordance with paragraph 1 of the present article shall enter into force when it has been approved by the General Assembly of the United Nations and accepted by a two-thirds majority of States Parties.

3. When an amendment enters into force, it shall be binding on those States Parties which have accepted it, other States Parties still being bound by the provisions of the present Convention and any earlier amendments which they have accepted.

Article 51
• •

1. The Secretary-General of the United Nations shall receive and circulate to all States the text of reservations made by States at the time of ratification or accession.

2. A reservation incompatible with the object and purpose of the present Convention shall not be permitted.

3. Reservations may be withdrawn at any time by notification to that effect addressed to the Secretary-General of the United Nations, who shall then inform all States. Such notification shall take effect on the date on which it is received by the Secretary-General.

Article 52
• •

A State Party may denounce the present Convention by written notification to the Secretary-General of the United Nations. Denunciation becomes effective one year after the date of receipt of the notification by the Secretary-General.

Article 53

The Secretary-General of the United Nations is designated as the depositary of the present Convention.

Article 54

The original of the present Convention, of which the Arabic, Chinese, English, French, Russian and Spanish texts are equally authentic, shall be deposited with the SecretaryGeneral of the Unit United Nations.

In witness thereof the undersigned plenipotentiaries, being duly authorized thereto by their respective Governments, have signed the present Convention.

A brief introduction to international human rights law terminology

*Excerpt from: Human Rights:
A Basic Handbook for UN Staff,
pp. 2-5*

Human rights are commonly understood as being those rights which are inherent to the human being. The concept of human rights acknowledges that every single human being is entitled to enjoy his or her human rights without distinction as to race, colour, sex, language, religion, political or other opinion, national or social origin, property, birth or other status.

Human rights are legally guaranteed by *human rights law,* protecting individuals and groups against actions that interfere with fundamental freedoms and human dignity. They are expressed in treaties, customary international law, bodies of principles and other sources of law. Human rights law places an obligation on States to act in a particular way and prohibits States from engaging in specified activities. However, the law does not establish human rights. Human rights are inherent entitlements which come to every person as a consequence of being human. Treaties and other sources of law generally serve to *protect* formally the rights of individuals and groups against actions or abandonment of actions by Governments which interfere with the enjoyment of their human rights.

The following are some of the most important characteristics of human rights:

- Human rights are founded on *respect for the dignity and worth of each person;*
- Human rights are *universal,* meaning that they are applied equally and without discrimination to all people;
- Human rights are *inalienable,* in that no one can have his or her human rights taken away; they can be limited in specific situations (for example, the right to liberty can be restricted if a person is found guilty of a crime by a court of law);
- Human rights are *indivisible, interrelated* and *interdependent,* for the reason that it is insufficient to respect some human rights and not others. In practice, the violation of one right will often affect respect for several other rights. All human rights should therefore be seen as having equal importance and of being equally essential to respect for the dignity and worth of every person.

International human rights law

The formal expression of inherent human rights is through *international human rights law.* A series of international human rights treaties and other instruments have emerged since 1945 conferring legal form on inherent human rights. The creation of the United Nations provided an ideal forum for the development and adoption of international human rights instruments. Other instruments have been adopted at a regional level reflecting the particular human rights concerns of the region. Most States have also adopted constitutions and other laws which formally protect basic human rights. Often the language used by States is drawn directly from the international human rights instruments.

International human rights law consists mainly of treaties and custom as well as, inter alia, declarations, guidelines and principles.

Treaties

A treaty is an agreement by States to be bound by particular rules. International treaties have different designations such as *covenants, charters, protocols, conventions, accords* and *agreements.* A treaty is legally binding on those States which have consented to be bound by the provisions of the treaty – in other words are *party* to the treaty.

A State can become a *party* to a treaty by *ratification, accession* or *succession. Ratification* is a State's formal expression of consent to be bound by a treaty. Only a State that has previously signed the treaty (during the period when the treaty was open for signature) can ratify it. Ratification consists of two procedural acts: on the domestic level, it requires approval by the appropriate constitutional organ (usually the head of State or parliament). On the international level, pursuant to the relevant provision of the treaty in question, the instrument of ratification shall be formally transmitted to the depositary which may be a State or an international organization such as the United Nations.

Accession entails consent to be bound by a State that has not previously signed the instrument. States ratify treaties both before and after the treaty has entered into force. The same applies to accession.

A State may also become party to a treaty by *succession,* which takes place by virtue of a specific treaty provision or by declaration.

Most treaties are not self-executing. In some States treaties are superior to domestic law, whereas in other States treaties are given constitutional status, and in yet others only certain provisions of a treaty are incorporated in domestic law.

A State may, in ratifying a treaty, enter reservations to that treaty, indicating that, while it consents to be bound by most of the provisions, it does not agree to be bound by certain specific provisions. However, a reservation may not defeat the object and purpose of the treaty. Further, even if a State is not a party to a treaty or if it has entered reservations thereto, that State may still be bound by those treaty provisions which have become part of customary international law or constitute peremptory rules of international law, such as the prohibition against torture.

Custom

Customary international law (or simply "custom") is the term used to describe a general and consistent practice followed by States deriving from a sense of legal obligation. Thus, for example, while the Universal Declaration of Human Rights is not in itself a binding treaty, some of its provisions have the character of customary international law.

Declarations, resolutions etc. adopted by United Nations organs

General norms of international law – principles and practices that most States would agree on – are often stated in *declarations, proclamations, standard rules, guidelines, recommendations* and *principles.* While no binding legal effect on States ensues, they nevertheless represent a broad consensus on the part of the international community and, therefore, have a strong and undeniable moral force in terms of the practice of

States in their conduct of international relations. The value of such instruments rests on their recognition and acceptance by a large number of States, and, even without binding legal effect, they may be seen as declaratory of broadly accepted principles within the international community.

Annex 4

Selected organizations

United Nations organizations

Organizations within the United Nations system can provide materials and other forms of support for human rights education programmes. The addresses of the headquarters of a selected list of United Nations organizations follow; they will be able to provide details regarding their national presences/counterparts.

Office of the United Nations High Commissioner for Human Rights (OHCHR)

United Nations Decade for Human Rights Education (1995-2004)
Palais des Nations
1211 Geneva 10
SWITZERLAND
Tel: +41 22 917 92 69
Fax: +41 22 917 90 03
E-mail: hredatabase@ohchr.org
Web site: http://www.ohchr.org

United Nations Educational, Scientific, and Cultural Organization (UNESCO)

Education Sector
7, place de Fontenoy
75352 Paris 07 SP
FRANCE
Tel: +33 1 45 68 10 00
Fax: +33 1 45 67 16 90
E-mail: webmaster@unesco.org
Web site: http://www.unesco.org

UNESCO International Bureau of Education

15, route des Morillons
1218 Grand-Saconnex
Geneva
SWITZERLAND
Tel: +41 22 917 78 00
Fax: +41 22 917 78 01
E-mail: doc.centre@ibe.unesco.org
Web site: http://www.ibe.unesco.org

United Nations Children's Fund (UNICEF)

UNICEF House
3, United Nations Plaza
New York, N.Y. 10017, USA
Tel: +1 212 326 7000
Fax: +1 212 887 7465 / 887 7454
E-mail: info@unicef.org
Web site: http://www.unicef.org

UNICEF Innocenti Research Centre

Piazza SS. Annunziata 12
50122 Florence, ITALY
Tel: +39 055 20 33 0
Fax: +39 055 24 48 17
E-mail: florence@unicef.org
Web site: http://www.unicef-icdc.org

United Nations Department of Public Information (DPI)

United Nations Cyberschoolbus
c/o Global Teaching and Learning Project
United Nations Headquarters
New York, NY 10017
USA
Tel: +1 212 963 8589
Fax: +1 212 963 0071
E-mail: cyberschoolbus@un.org
Web site:
http://www.un.org/cyberschoolbus

United Nations Development Programme (UNDP)

1, United Nations Plaza
New York, N.Y. 10017
USA
Tel: +1 212 906 5558
Fax: +1 212 906 5364
E-mail: enquiries@undp.org
Web site: http://www.undp.org

Food and Agriculture Organization of the United Nations (FAO)

Viale delle Terme di Caracalla
00100 Rome
ITALY
Tel: +39 06 5705 1
Fax +39 06 5705 3152
E-mail: FAO-HQ@fao.org
Web site: http://www.fao.org

International Labour Organization (ILO)

4, route des Morillons
1211 Geneva 22
SWITZERLAND
Tel: +41 22 799 61 11
Fax: +41 22 798 86 85
E-mail: ilo@ilo.org
Web site: http://www.ilo.org

United Nations Environment Programme (UNEP)

United Nations Avenue, Gigiri
P.O. Box 30552
Nairobi
KENYA
Tel: +254 2 621234
Fax: +254 2 624489/90
E-mail: eisinfo@unep.org
Web site: http://www.unep.org

Office of the United Nations High Commissioner for Refugees (UNHCR)

P.O. Box 2500
1211 Genève 2 Dépôt
SWITZERLAND
Tel.: +41 22 739 81 11
Fax +41 22 739 73 77
E-mail: webmaster@unhcr.ch
Web site: http://www.unhcr.ch

World Health Organization (WHO)

20, Avenue Appia
1211 Geneva 27
SWITZERLAND
Tel: +41 22 791 21 11
Fax +41 22 791 31 11
E-mail: info@who.int
Web site: http://www.who.int

Other organizations

The following organizations provide primary, middle and secondary school educators with information, conference facilities, training and materials about human rights education. For complete and current information on their activities and resources, contact these organizations or visit their web sites on the Internet.[a]

International level

Most of these organizations have national chapters or counterparts, which carry out human rights education programmes and develop related materials. Information on national contacts can be obtained at the following addresses.

**Amnesty International
Human Rights Education Team
International Secretariat**

1 Easton Street
London WC1X 0DW
UNITED KINGDOM
Tel: +44 207 4135513
Fax: +44 207 9561157
E-mail: hreteam@amnesty.org
Web site: http://www.amnesty.org

> *Has extensive programmes and resources for human rights education, including a regularly updated annotated bibliography of resources in many languages that is available online at: <http://www.amnesty.org> [search under "Library" ? "View by theme" ? "Human rights education"].*

---

[a] For a broad listing of related organizations, see also: "*The Human Rights Education Resourcebook*", second edition, Human Rights Education Associates (HREA), 2000. Available on-line at <http://www.hrea.org>.

Anti-Slavery International
Thomas Clarkson House,
The Stableyard, Broomgrove Road
London SW9 9TL, UNITED KINGDOM
Tel: +44 20 7501 8920
Fax: +44 20 7738 4110
E-mail: info@antislavery.org
Web site: http://www.antislavery.org
> Publishes resources for use in schools
and offers education programmes
on human rights in schools and
youth centres. Breaking the Silence
is an educational resources web site
on the transatlantic slave trade.

**Association mondiale pour l'école
instrument de paix/World
Association for the School as an
Instrument of Peace (EIP)**
5, rue de Simplon
1207 Geneva, SWITZERLAND
Tel: +41 22 735 2422
Fax: +41 22 735 0653
E-mail: cifedhop@mail-box.ch
Web site: http://www.eip-
cifedhop.org
> Publishes materials for use in schools
and provides training, including a
summer course for teachers with
French, English, and Spanish sections.

Canadian Human Rights Foundation
1425 René-Lévesque Blvd. West,
Suite 407
Montréal, Québec, Canada H3G 1T7
CANADA
Tel: +1 514 9540382
Fax: +1 514 9540659
E-mail: chrf@chrf.ca
Web site: http://www.chrf.ca
> Provides curriculum materials and
offers regional training programmes
in Africa, Asia and Central and
Eastern Europe. It offers a summer
International Human Rights Training
Programme (IHRTP) for educators
and activists.

Cultural Survival
215 Prospect Street
Cambridge, MA 02139, USA

Tel: +1 617 441 5400
Fax: +1 617 441 5417
E-mail: csinc@cs.org
Web site: http://www.cs.org
> Provides materials and training on
indigenous rights worldwide.

Education International
5 bd du Roi Albert II
1210 Brussels
BELGIUM
Tel: +32 2 224 0611
Fax: +32 2 224 0606
E-mail: headoffice@ei-ie.org
Web site: http://www.ei-ie.org
> A worldwide trade union
organization of education personnel
working in all sectors of education
from pre-school to university.

**Human Rights Education Associates
(HREA)**
HREA - USA Office
P.O. Box 382396
Cambridge, MA 02238, USA
Tel: +1 617 6250278
Fax: +1 617 2490278
E-mail: info@hrea.org
Web site: http://www.hrea.org
> Provides extensive resources to
educators, including consultation in
curriculum and materials
development, programme
evaluation, an online Resource
Centre for Human Rights Education
and an international list-serv for
human rights educators.

**International Committee of the Red
Cross (ICRC)**
19, avenue de la Paix
1202 Geneva, SWITZERLAND
Tel: +41 22 734 6001
Fax: +41-22 733 2057
E-mail: webmaster.gva@icrc.org
Web site: http://www.icrc.org
> Its mandate includes the
dissemination of international law of
armed conflict and human rights law
through education, training and
public awareness.

International Helsinki Federation for Human Rights (IFHR)
Wickenburgg. 14/7
1080 Vienna, AUSTRIA
Tel: +43 1 408 8822
Fax: +43 1 408 882250
E-mail: office@ihf-hr.org
Web site: http://www.ihf-hr.org
> *Although principally concerned with monitoring and reporting, many national Helsinki Committees also provide human rights education materials and training.*

International Save the Children Alliance
275-281 King Street
London W6 9LZ
UNITED KINGDOM
Tel: +44 20 8748 2554
Fax: +44 20 8237 8000
E-mail: Infor@save-children-alliance.org
Web site:
http://www.savethechildren.net
> *Educates and advocates on the rights of the child.*

OXFAM International
International Secretariat
Suite 20, 266 Banbury Road
Oxford, OX2 7DL
UNITED KINGDOM
Tel: +44 1865 31 3939
Fax: +44 1865 31 3770
E-mail:
information@oxfaminternational.org
Web site:
http://www.oxfaminternational.org
> *Educational focus is on the right to development, gender issues and social and economic rights.*

Peace Child International
The White House
Buntingford, Herts. SG9 9AH
UNITED KINGDOM
Tel: +44 176 327 4459
Fax: +44 176 327 4460
E-mail: webmaster@peacechild.org
Web site: http://www.peacechild.org

> *A network of high-school student groups in more than 100 countries, run by young people in partnership with adult professionals.*

People's Movement for Human Rights Education (PDHRE)
526 W. 111th Street
New York, NY 10025
USA
Tel: +1 212 749 3156
Fax: +1 212 666 6325
E-mail: pdhre@igc.apc.org
Web site: http://www.pdhre.org
> *A resource centre for research and development of educational materials with online resources.*

World Federation of United Nations Associations (WFUNA/FMANU)
c/o Palais des Nations
1211 Geneva 10
SWITZERLAND
Tel: +44 22 917 3213/3239
Fax: +44 22 917 0185
E-mail: wfuna@unog.ch
Web site: http://www.wfuna.org
> *Many United Nations Associations develop training programmes and materials about human rights for use in formal education, including model United Nations programmes.*

World Organization of the Scout Movement (World Scout Bureau)
P.O. Box 241
1211 Geneva 4
SWITZERLAND
Tel: +41 22 705 1010
Fax: +41 22 705 1020
E-mail:
worldbureau@world.scout.org
Web site: http://www.scout.org
> *Includes educational programmes and materials on development and children rights.*

Some contacts at the regional level

Africa and the Middle East

African Centre for Democracy and Human Rights Studies (ACDHRS)
Zoe Tembo Building,
Kerr Sereign K. S. M. D.
P. O. Box: 2728
Serrekunda, GAMBIA
Tel: +220 462340 / 462341/ 462342
Fax: +220 462338 / 462339
E-mail: acdhrs@acdhrs.org or
info@acdhrs.org
Web site: http://www.acdhrs.org
> Main activities include training, information and documentation in the field of human rights. Produces material for human rights education in schools.

Cairo Institute for Human Rights Studies (CIHRS)
P.O. Box 117
Maglis el-Shaab
11516 Cairo, EGYPT
Tel: +202 7946065
Fax: +202 7921913
E-mail: cihrs@soficom.com.eg
Web site: http://www.cihrs.org
> Provides human rights training and publications for students and educators.

Centre for Socio-Legal Studies (CSLS)
University of Natal
Durban 4014 SOUTH AFRICA
Tel: +27 31 260 1291
Fax: +27 31 260 1540
E-mail: degrandprei@nu.ac.za
Web site: http://www.csls.org.za
Coordinates the Street Law and Democracy for All programmes. Offers teacher training and curriculum materials.

Institut Arabe des Droits de l'Homme (IADH) / Arab Institute for Human Rights (AIHR)
14 Rue Al-Jahidh, Menzahl
1004 Tunis, TUNISIA

Tel: +216 1 767 003/ 767 889
Fax: +216 1 750 911
E-mail : aihr.infocenter@gnet.tn
Web site: http://www.aihr.org.tn
> Develops training programmes and materials for teachers, students and children.

Institute for Democracy in South Africa (IDASA)
357 Visagie Street (corner Prinsloo)
PO Box 56950, Arcadia Pretoria 0007
SOUTH AFRICA
Tel: +27 12 392 0500
Fax: +27 12 320 2414/5
E-mail: marie@idasa.org.za
Web site: http://www.idasa.org.za
> Develops materials and provides teacher training at the secondary school level.

Union Interafricaine des Droits de l'Homme (UIDH)
01 BP 1346 - Ouagadougou
BURKINA FASO
Tel: +226 31 61 45
Fax: +226 31 61 44
E-mail: uidh@fasonet.bf
Web site:
http://www.hri.ca/partners/uidh
> Conducts human rights education programmes at the regional level.

Asia and the Pacific[b]

Asian Regional Resource Center for Human Rights Education (ARRC)
2738 Ladprao 128/3
Klongchan, Bangkapi
Bangkok 10240, THAILAND
Tel: +662 731 0829/ 377 5641
Fax: +662 731 0829
E-mail: arrc@ksc.th.com
Web site: www.arrc-hre.com

---

[b] For a more complete listing, see A Directory of Asian and the Pacific Organizations Related to Human Rights Education Work, third edition, Asian Regional Resource Center for Human Rights Education (ARRC), January 2003. Available on-line at: < www.arrc-hre.com >.

> *A comprehensive centre providing materials and training for both formal and non-formal human rights education throughout Asia.*

Asia-Pacific Human Rights Information Center (HURIGHTS OSAKA)
1-2-1-1500, Benten, Minato-ku
Osaka-shi, Osaka 552-0007
JAPAN
Tel: +81 6 6577 3578
Fax: +81 6 6577 3583
E-mail: webmail@hurights.or.jp
Web site: http://www.hurights.or.jp
> *A resource and documentation centre with programmes in both formal and non-formal education.*

Human Rights Correspondence School
c/o Asian Human Rights Commission
Unit D, 7/F., Mongkok Commercial Center,
16-16B Argyle Street, Kowloon
Hong Kong
CHINA
Tel: +852 2698 6339
Fax: +852 2698 6367
E-mail: hrschool@ahrchk.org or
support@hrschool.org
Web site: http://www.hrschool.org
supahrchk.net
> *A web site with documents, information and materials to facilitate the development of human rights education modules in Asian countries.*

Philippines Normal University - Gender, Peace and Human Rights Education
Taft Avenue
1001 Manila
PHILIPPINES
Tel: +63 2 5244032
Fax: +63 2 5270372
E-mail: yeban@compass.com.ph
> *Trains teachers in pedagogy and curriculum development for human rights education.*

South Asian Human Rights Documentation Center
B-6/6, Safdarjang Enclave Extension
New Delhi 110029, INDIA
Tel: +91 11 619 1120/ 619 2717
Fax : +91 11 619 1120
E-mail: hrdc_online@hotmail.com
Web site:
http://hri.ca/partners/sahrdc
> *Develops curricula for the teaching of human rights in schools.*

America

Human Rights Center
University of Minnesota
Mondale Hall, N-120
229-19th Avenue South
Minneapolis, MN 55455, USA
Tel: +1 612 626 0041
Fax: +1 612 625 2011
E-mail: humanrts@umn.edu
Web sites: http://www.hrusa.org
> *Provides comprehensive services to educators, including training, publications and both direct and online information; publishes the Human Rights Education Series; offers a summer training-of-trainers course.*

Instituto Interamericano de Derechos Humanos (IIDH)
Apartado 10081-1000
San José, COSTA RICA
Tel: +506 234 0404
Fax: +506 234 0955
E-mail: instituto@iidh.ed.cr
Web site: http://www.iidh.ed.cr
> *A comprehensive centre whose work includes developing materials and conducting training for secondary school teachers.*

Instituto Peruano de Educación en Derechos Humanos y la Paz (IPEDEHP)
Los Gavilanes 195 San Isidro
Lima 11, PERU
Tel: +51 1 2215713/ 2215668/
4414602
Fax: +51 1 4606759

E-mail: ipedehp@dhperu.org
Web site: http://www.human-rights.
net/IPEDEHP
> *Publishes a wide range of
materials for schools and
provides training courses for
teachers.*

**Network of Educators on
the Americas (NECA)**
P.O. Box 73038
Washington, DC 20056
USA
Tel: +1 202 588 7204 (toll free: +1
800 763 9131)
Fax: +1 202 238 0109
E-mail: necadc@aol.com
Web site:
http://www.teachingforchange.org
> *Provides teacher training and an
extensive catalogue of materials
on social justice issues in English
and Spanish.*

**Red Latinoamericana de Educación
para la Paz y los Derechos Humanos**
c/o Red de Apoyo por la Justicia
y la Paz
Parque Central, Edificio Caroata
Nivel Oficina 2, Oficina n. 220
Caracas 1015-A
VENEZUELA
Tel/Fax: +58 212 5741949/ 5748005
E-mail: redapoyo@cantv.net
> *A coalition of more than
30 organizations in Latin
America and the Caribbean
dealing with human rights
education.*
Servicio Paz y Justicia (SERPAJ)

Joaquín Requena 1642
CP 11 200
Montevideo
URUGUAY
Tel: +598 2 408 5301
Fax: +598 2 408 5701
E-mail: serpajuy@serpaj.org.uy
Web site: http://www.serpaj.org.uy
> *Provides teacher training and
materials for formal education.*

Southern Poverty Law Centre
400 Washington Avenue
Montgomery, Alabama 36104
USA
Tel: +1 334 956 8200
Fax: +1 334-956 8488
Web site: http://www.splcenter.org
> *Provides educational materials
online for teachers, parents and
students to combat hate,
discrimination and intolerance.*

Street Law, Inc.
1600 K Street NW., Suite 602
Washington, DC 20006
USA
Tel: +1 202 293 0088
Fax: +1 202 293 0089
E-mail: clearinghouse@streetlaw.org
Web site: http://www.streetlaw.org
> *Provides curriculum materials and
training for teachers and secondary
students for use in educating the
community about law, human rights,
democracy and conflict resolution.*

Europe

**Center for Citizenship
Education/Centrum Edukacji
Obywatelskiej**
Ul. Willowa 9/3
00-790 Warszawa, POLAND
Tel/Fax: +48 22 646 2025
E-mail: ceo@ceo.org.pl
Web site: http://www.ceo.org.pl
> *Provides teaching materials and
training for secondary school
students, teachers and
administrators.*

**Centre for Citizenship Studies in
Education**
School of Education
University of Leicester
21 University Road
Leicester, LE1 7RF
UNITED KINGDOM
Tel: +44 116 252 3681
Fax: +44 116 252 3653
E-mail: ccse@le.ac.uk

Web site:
http://www.le.ac.uk/education/centres/citizenship
> *Works in partnership with schools to promote research and education for citizenship, human rights and the teaching of democracy in schools; has a distance learning programme in human rights education.*

Centre for Global Education
York St. John College
Lord Mayor's Walk
York Y031 7EX
UNITED KINGDOM
Tel: +44 1904 716839/716825
Fax: +44 1904 612512
E-mail: global.ed@dial.pipex.com
Web site: http://www.yorksj.ac.uk
(search under "About us" ?
"Centres")
> *Offers materials and training, including an annual summer school; publishes the Human Rights Education Newsletter.*

Citizenship Foundation
Ferroners House
Shaftesbury Place, Aldersgate Street
London EC2Y 8AA
UNITED KINGDOM
Tel: +44 020 7367 0500
Fax: +44 020 7367 0501
E-mail: info@citfou.org.uk
Web site: http://www.citfou.org.uk/
> *Provides materials, curriculum development and teacher training in the UK and Central and Eastern Europe.*

Council of Europe
67075 Strasbourg Cedex, FRANCE
Tel: +33 388 412 033
Fax: +33 388 412 745
E-mail: infopoint@coe.int
Web site: http://www.coe.int
> *Publishes extensive resources for human rights education in French and English, especially relating to tolerance and the European Convention on Human Rights.*

North-South Centre - European Centre for Global Interdependence and Solidarity
Avenida da Libertade 229/4o
1250-142 Lisbon
PORTUGAL
Tel: +351 21 358 40 58
Fax: +351 21 352 49 66/ 21 358 40 37
E-mail: nscinfo@coe.int
Web site: http://www.nscentre.org
> *Develops materials and publishes a monthly newsletter.*

Annex 5

Other selected classroom resources[a]

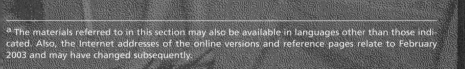

---

[a] The materials referred to in this section may also be available in languages other than those indicated. Also, the Internet addresses of the online versions and reference pages relate to February 2003 and may have changed subsequently.

United Nations resources

All human beings ... Manual for human rights education (UNESCO, Education Sector, 1998)

Languages: Albanian, Arabic, English, French.
Online version (Arabic, English, French): available on payment of a fee at http://upo.unesco.org/booksonline.asp

> An illustrated practical guide to help primary and secondary school students and teachers understand the universal elements of human rights. It aims to promote the common aspiration to social progress and better living conditions in a context of greater freedom, as laid down in the Universal Declaration of Human Rights. It does not seek to be exhaustive, but rather to propose material that educators and learners can develop and adapt to their own cultural contexts.

Education for Development: A Teacher's Resource for Global Learning by Susan Fountain (UNICEF, Education for Development Section, 1995)

Languages: English, French.
Online reference page: http://www.unicef.org/pubsgen/edu-develop/index.html

> Aims at helping young people make the link between global issues and local concerns and showing how they can apply what they learn to their own lives and communities. Also provides teachers of all subjects and at all levels with practical classrooms activities that can be integrated into existing curricula.

Human Rights: Questions and Answers by Leah Levin (UNESCO, Education Sector, 1996)

Languages: Albanian, Arabic, Armenian, Belarusian, Danish, English, Finnish, French, German, Greek, Indonesian, Japanese, Portuguese, Swedish, Slovak, Spanish, Russian.
Online version (English, French, Spanish): available on payment of a fee at http://upo.unesco.org/booksonline.asp

> Provides basic information on major human rights instruments, procedures for their implementation and activities of international organizations to promote and protect human rights. The first part describes the scope and meaning of international human rights law, especially the development of protection procedures and the importance of human rights education. The second part explains the meaning of each of the thirty articles of the Universal Declaration of Human Rights.

It's Only Right! – A Practical Guide to Learning About the Convention on the Rights of the Child by Susan Fountain (UNICEF, Education for Development Section, 1993)

Languages: English, French.
Online version (English): http://www.unicef.org/teachers/protection/only_right.htm

> For the sake of both individual and global development, children around the world need to understand the concept of rights, to know the rights to which they are entitled, to empathize with those whose rights have been denied, and to be empowered to take action on behalf on their own rights and those of others. Learning about the Convention on the Rights of the Child through this Guide is one way to begin.

Primary School Kit on the United Nations / Intermediate School Kit on the United Nations / Secondary School Kit on the United Nations (United Nations, 1995)

Languages: English, French, Spanish, Thai.

Online version (English):
http://www0.un.org/cyberschoolbus/
bookstor/kits/english

Online version (French):
http://www0.un.org/cyberschoolbus/
bookstor/kits/french

Online version (Spanish):
http://www0.un.org/cyberschoolbus/
bookstor/kits/spanish

> Published on the fiftieth anniversary
of the United Nations, these kits offer
teachers and students of every
subject a way to explore global issues
by linking their lives to the vast but
connected world around them.
Valuable curriculum enrichment
packages cover topics ranging from
pollution to peacekeeping, from
decolonization to development.
Science and mathematics teachers as
well as history and social science
teachers will find units that fit easily
into their curricula. Each unit includes
a main text that reviews the topics, a
UN factfile that presents specific
examples of United Nations
involvement, and activities that
encourage critical and creative
thinking, participation and reflection
on one's own attitude and behaviour.
In addition to being sources of
information, the units also
demonstrate how an international
organization can improve life for
citizens of all countries.

Tolerance: the threshold of peace by
Betty A. Reardon (UNESCO,
Education Sector, 1997)

Languages: Albanian, English,
French, Spanish.

Online version (English):
http://www.unesco.org/education/
pdf/34_57.pdf

Online version (French):
http://www.unesco.org/education/
pdf/34_57_f.pdf

Online version (Spanish):
http://www.unesco.org/education/pd
f/34_57_s.pdf

This publication is composed of 3
units:
- Teacher-training resource unit
- Primary-school resource unit
- Secondary-school resource unit

> How can tolerance be a key word in
the educational process? How can
educators be helped to identify
problems related to intolerance as
soon as they are witnessed and
formulate objectives adapted to
their community and to their
students? How can students be
taught to accept human diversity, to
manage conflicts and to act
responsibly? The three units of this
book, respectively aimed at
teachers/educators, elementary
schools and secondary schools,
attempt to answer these questions
with selected study materials.
Tolerance is placed in the framework
of education for peace, human
rights and democracy through many
sample activities and themes for
study and reflection. These books
are addressed to teachers, as well as
teacher trainers, community actors,
parents and social workers – in sum,
to all those whose educational
mission can contribute to opening a
door onto peace.

UN Cyberschoolbus (web site)

Address:
http://www.un.org/cyberschoolbus
Languages: Arabic, Chinese, English,
French, Russian, Spanish.

> The United Nations Cyberschoolbus
was created in 1996 as the online
education component of the Global
Teaching and Learning Project,
whose mission is to promote
education about international issues
and the United Nations. The Global
Teaching and Learning Project
produces teaching materials and
activities designed for students and
teachers at primary, intermediate
and secondary school level. This
project aims at providing both

online and print educational resources for an increasingly globalized world.

UNICEF Teachers Talking about Learning (web site)

Address: http://www.unicef.org/teachers
Language: English.

> "Teachers Talking about Learning" has been designed to support the professional development of teachers and educators, and to assist them with practical advice related to resources, classroom activities and other information to develop child-friendly learning environments. The site is structured around three main sections:
> • Explore ideas by reading and reflection;
> • Discuss issues by talking with peers; and
> • Take action by doing activities.

UNICEF Voices of Youth (web site)

Address: http://www.unicef.org/voy
Languages: English, French, Spanish.

> This site invites young visitors to discuss ways in which the world can become a place where the rights of every child are protected, that is, the right to live in peace, to have decent shelter, to be healthy and well-nourished, to have clean water, to play, to go to school, and to be protected from violence, abuse and exploitation. Provides an opportunity to think about and give views on current global issues, a series of interactive global learning projects and a forum for teachers, trainers and educational planners.

Other resources

Carpeta Latinoamericana de Materiales Didácticos para Educación en Derechos Humanos (Instituto Interamericano de Derechos Humanos/ Centro de Recursos Educativos – Amnistía Internacional, 1995)

Language: Spanish.
Online reference page: http://www.iidh.ed.cr/publicaciones/listadoPubs.asp

> The general objective of the three pedagogical units (freedom, equality, solidarity and participation) is to provide support for educators and propose a methodology for human rights education in order to reinforce the learning process through practical activities for educators as well as students.

Educating for Human Dignity – Learning about Rights and Responsibilities by Betty A. Reardon (University of Pennsylvania Press, 1995)

Language: English.
Online reference page: http://www.upenn.edu/pennpress/book/1559.html

> This book is written for both teachers and teacher educators. It is a resource offering both guidance and support materials for human rights education programmes from kindergarten through high school. It opens possibilities for a holistic approach to human rights education that directly confronts the values issues raised by human rights problems in a context of global interrelationships. The conceptual development approach used throughout the book makes it suitable for a full human rights curriculum; the grade-level discussions and sample lesson plans can be used in individual classes or to enrich ongoing programmes.

First Steps – A Manual for Starting Human Rights Education (Amnesty International, 1996)

Languages: Albanian, Arabic, Dutch, English, Hungarian, Polish, Portuguese, Russian, Slovak, Slovenian, Ukrainian.
Online version (English and other languages):
http://web.amnesty.org/web/web.nsf/pages/hre_first

> This manual is for teachers and others who work with young people and who want to introduce human rights into their educational practices. It is designed to be a basic introduction, with age-specific activities for younger and older children. There is also advice on methodology and help for those who want to go further into this subject. The approach stresses the practical rather than the theoretical. The intention is that educators can take this material and adapt it to suit their own circumstances and context.

An adaptation of this manual for Africa is entitled Siniko: Towards a Human Rights Culture in Africa (Amnesty International, 1998), available in English, French and Swahili.
Online version:
http://web.amnesty.org/web/web.nsf/pages/hre_res

Human Rights for All by Edward L. O'Brien, Eleanor Greene and David McQuoidMason (National Institute for Citizen Education in the Law, 1996)

Languages: English, Hungarian, Romanian, Russian, Spanish.
Online reference page:
http://www.streetlaw.org/pubs.html

> This book is meant for use in middle and secondary schools. Adults interested in learning the basics of human rights as part of a course or just through informal education or reading can also use it. The text of the book does not make reference to any specific country by name, as the authors believe that human rights are universal and apply to the lives of everyone in every country. However, those familiar with human rights will recognize that many of the scenarios were taken from events which occurred in various parts of the world.

Human Rights Here and Now: Celebrating the Universal Declaration of Human Rights edited by Nancy Flowers (Human Rights Resource Center, University of Minnesota, 1998)

Languages: English, Spanish.
Online version (English):
http://www1.umn.edu/humanrts/edumat/hreduseries/hereandnow/Default.htm

> This book is intended for use by both community groups and teachers in elementary and secondary schools, and constitutes a "starter kit" for human rights education, with background information on human rights history, principles and issues; activities for a wide variety of age groups, from kindergarten through adult groups; and essential human rights documents.

Our World, Our Rights – Teaching about Rights and Responsibilities in Primary School edited by Margot Brown (Amnesty International United Kingdom, 1996)

Languages: English, Mongolian.
Online reference page:
http://www.amnesty.org.uk/action/tan/resources.shtml#our

> This book is designed to introduce primary-age children to the Universal Declaration of Human Rights. It offers children a simple way of understanding the rights embodied in the Declaration and what they look like in their lives;

and also helps them to identify what a right is – and the responsibilities that accompany it, as well as what action they might take to defend their rights and those of others.

Popular Education for Human Rights by Richard Pierre Claude (Human Rights Education Associates, 2000)

Languages: English, Chinese, Indonesian, Spanish.
Online version (English):
http://www.hrea.org/pubs/Popular_Education
Earlier version: The Bells of Freedom, in Amharic, English, French.
Online version (English):
http://www1.umn.edu/humanrts/education/belfry.pdf
Online version (French):
http://www.hrea.org/erc/Library/Bells_of_Freedom/index_fr.html

> This book is a trainer's guide for human rights activists. It is deliberately not copyrighted in solidarity with those involved in popular education and community organizing; any non-governmental organization or educator may copy and adapt it to local settings and culture simply by acknowledging the author and source. Designed for non-formal education, the manual gives teachers options that are appropriate for participants with minimal literacy skills. The emphasis is on the concerns of marginalized groups including the rural poor, women and children. The participatory exercises can also be used in formal education.

Stand up NOW for Human Rights! (video and support pack), (Council of Europe, 1997)

Languages: English and various other European languages.

> This video aims at raising human rights awareness among young people, primarily in the age group 13 to 18, by explaining the historical development of human rights and

showing how young people can be involved in activities to protect and promote human rights through Europe. The video is accompanied by a support pack, explaining how the video can be used for educational purposes.

The European Convention on Human Rights: Starting Points for Teachers (Council of Europe, 2000)

Languages: English, French, German.
Online version (English):
http://www.coe.int/portalT.asp
Online version (French):
http://www.coe.int/portailT.asp
(go to General Information -> Information Material -> Human Rights Fact Sheet)

> This teaching kit is composed of two series of teaching materials: one on the elaboration of the European Convention for the Protection of Human Rights and Fundamental Freedoms, the other one on the content of the Convention. This last part consists of sheets presenting activities which can be organized in the classroom and which address various subjects such as the content and meaning of human rights, national human rights protection systems, human rights at school, etc. Teachers will find a list of activities and studies to be conducted with students: research on the Internet, interviews, viewing of films addressing human rights issues, etc.

Stand up for your rights – A book about human rights written, illustrated and edited by young people of the world (Peace Child International, 1998)

Language: English.
Online reference page:
http://www.peacechild.org/acatalog

> This book is a commentary written by children and young people on the Universal Declaration on Human Rights. Stories, poems, personal recollections and illustrations help to

bring each article of the Declaration to life. There are also details on organizations to join and things to do to help make the world a better place. A teacher's guide is also available.

Other selected classroom resources

Printed at United Nations, Geneva
GE.04-42997 — August 2004 — 8,660
Reprinted at United Nations, Geneva
GE.05-81552 — November 2005 — 5,000
GE.07-82547 — August 2007 — 4,000
GE.10-80440 — April 2010 — 5,000

HR/PUB/2004/2

United Nations publication
Sales No. E.03.XIV.3
ISBN 92-1-154149-2